★ The War on Terrorism ★

THE WAR IN AFGHANISTAN

Titles in the American War Library series include:

The War on Terrorism
Combating the Global Terrorist Threat
Leaders and Generals
Life of an American Soldier in Afghanistan
The War at Home
Weapons of War

The American Revolution

The Civil War

The Cold War

The Korean War

The Persian Gulf War

The Vietnam War

World War I

World War II

AMERICAN
WAR LIBRARY

★ ★ ★ ★

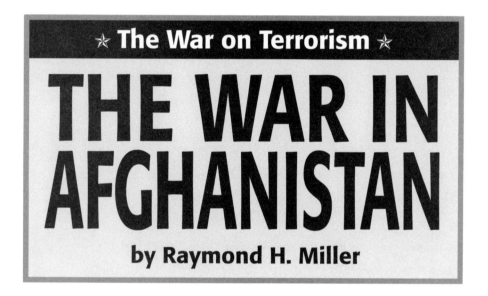

★ The War on Terrorism ★

THE WAR IN AFGHANISTAN

by Raymond H. Miller

LUCENT
BOOKS®

THOMSON

GALE

San Diego • Detroit • New York • San Francisco • Cleveland • New Haven, Conn. • Waterville, Maine • London • Munich

THOMSON

★

GALE

Cover: U.S. Army soldiers in full battle gear return to Bagram Air Base
after fighting al-Qaeda in the mountains of eastern Afghanistan.

© 2004 by Lucent Books. Lucent Books is an imprint of The Gale Group, Inc.,
a division of Thomson Learning, Inc.

Lucent Books® and Thomson Learning™ are trademarks used herein under license.

For more information, contact
Lucent Books
27500 Drake Rd.
Farmington Hills, MI 48331-3535
Or you can visit our Internet site at http://www.gale.com

LIBRARY OF CONGRESS CATALOGING-IN-PUBLICATION DATA

Miller, Raymond H.
   The war in Afghanistan / by Raymond H. Miller.
      v. cm. — (American war library. War on terrorism series)
Includes bibliographical references and index.
Contents: Afghanistan: A land of great chaos and conflict—Osama bin Laden and
al-Qaeda terror network—The United States mobilizes for war—Operation Enduring
Freedom begins with lightning air offenses—The sudden Taliban collapse—The hunt
for Osama bin Laden—The struggle for peace.
   ISBN 1-59018-331-2 (hardback : alk. paper)
   1. Afghanistan—History—2001—Juvenile literature. 2. War on Terrorism, 2001—
Juvenile literature. [1. Afghanistan—History—2001– 2. War on Terrorism, 2001–]
I. Title. II. Series.
   DS371.4.M55 2004
   958.104'6—dc22
                                                                    2003014494

★ Contents ★

A Nation Forged by War

The United States, like many nations, was forged and defined by war. Despite Benjamin Franklin's opinion that "There never was a good war or a bad peace," the United States owes its very existence to the War of Independence, one to which Franklin wholeheartedly subscribed. The country forged by war in 1776 was tempered and made stronger by the Civil War in the 1860s.

The Texas Revolution, the Mexican-American War, and the Spanish-American War expanded the country's borders and gave it overseas possessions. These wars made the United States a world power, but this status came with a price, as the nation became a key but reluctant player in both World War I and World War II.

Each successive war further defined the country's role on the world stage. Following World War II, U.S. foreign policy redefined itself to focus on the role of defender, not only of the freedom of its own citizens, but also of the freedom of people everywhere. During the Cold War that followed World War II until the collapse of the Soviet Union, defending the world meant fighting communism. This goal, manifested in the Korean and Vietnam conflicts, proved elusive, and soured the American public on its achievability. As the United States emerges as the world's sole superpower, American foreign policy has been guided less by national interest and more by protecting international human rights. But as involvement in Somalia and Kosovo proves, this goal has been equally elusive.

As a result, the country's view of itself changed. Bolstered by victories in World Wars I and II, Americans first relished the role of protector. But, as war followed war in a seemingly endless procession, Americans began to doubt their leaders, their motives, and themselves. The Vietnam War especially caused people to question the validity of sending its young people to die in places where they were not particularly wanted and for people who did not seem especially grateful.

While the most obvious changes brought about by America's wars have been geopolitical in nature, many other aspects of society have been touched. War often does not bring about change directly, but acts instead like the catalyst in a chemical reaction, accelerating changes already in progress.

Some of these changes have been societal. The role of women in the United States had been slowly changing, but World War II put thousands into the work force and into uniform. They might have gone back to being housewives after the war, but equality, once experienced, would not be forgotten.

Likewise, wars have accelerated technological change. The necessity for faster airplanes and more destructive bombs led to the development of jet planes and nuclear energy. Artificial fibers developed for parachutes in the 1940s were used in clothing of the 1950s.

Lucent Books' American War Library covers key wars in the development of the nation. Each war is covered in several volumes to allow for more detail, context, and to provide volumes on often neglected subjects, such as the kamikazes of World War II or the weapons used in the Civil War. As with all Lucent books, notes, annotated bibliographies, and appendixes such as glossaries give students a launching point for further research. In addition, sidebars and archival photographs enhance the text. Together, each volume in the American War Library will aid students in understanding how America's wars have shaped and changed its politics, economics, and society.

The First Battle in the War Against Terrorism

The United States and Afghanistan are not traditional enemies. They were allies of sorts in the Cold War era, particularly during the Soviet Union's military occupation of Afghanistan from 1979 to 1989, when the U.S. government supplied aid, training, and weapons to an Afghan resistance group known as the mujahideen (holy warriors). But when terrorists who had trained in Afghanistan hijacked four commercial airliners in the United States on September 11, 2001, and crashed them into the World Trade Center, the Pentagon, and a field in rural Pennsylvania, the remote Central Asian nation was thrust into the international spotlight and became the focus of the U.S.-led effort to stamp out terrorism.

The terrorists were members of al-Qaeda (roughly translated as "the Base"), a loose network of individuals and groups primarily from the Middle East. Led by a wealthy Saudi Arabian dissident named Osama bin Laden, al-Qaeda had operated in Afghanistan since 1996 under the protection of the ruling hard-line Islamic regime known as the Taliban. President George W. Bush called the coordinated strikes of September 11, which killed more than three thousand people, an act of war. He vowed, as commander in chief, to use any and all means necessary—including U.S. military force—to track down the culprits and bring them to justice.

The success or failure of the war against terrorism would have serious and direct implications for American citizens. If the military effort in Afghanistan proved to be ineffective, al-Qaeda would remain free to continue its aggression toward the United States, putting many more lives at risk. General Richard B. Myers, chairman of the Joint Chiefs of Staff, summarized the significance of this first war of the twenty-first century:

> I firmly believe that this [war against terrorism] is the most important task that the U.S. military has been handed since

the Second World War, and what's at stake here is no less than our freedom to exist as an American people. So there's no option but success. We owe it to our families and to the family of peace-loving nations to prevail in this fight.[1]

On October 7, 2001, less than one month after the terrorist attacks on America, President Bush launched Operation Enduring Freedom. Through the use of concentrated air strikes and a carefully coordinated ground assault, it took just over ninety days to liberate the Afghan people from the brutal Taliban regime. The fight against al-Qaeda forces and Taliban holdouts, however, proved to be a much more difficult endeavor. The United States was facing a new kind of enemy in Afghanistan, one that was largely unknown, unpredictable, and willing to die for its religious beliefs. From mountain hide-

U.S. soldiers transport bombs to be used in air strikes against al-Qaeda and Taliban targets in Afghanistan.

outs, al-Qaeda and Taliban fighters launched guerrilla-style attacks—the very tactics Afghan fighters had used to frustrate, and ultimately defeat, the Soviet Union two decades earlier.

Fighting against an elusive enemy required a different strategy than that which the Soviets had then employed and, indeed, the United States had used in previous wars. The massive, lumbering ground force that had typically been central to U.S. strategy in the past was largely absent in Afghanistan. Instead, small teams of highly mobile special operations forces took the leading role in combat. These commandos partnered on the ground with anti-Taliban Afghan soldiers

U.S. Navy SEALs conduct a reconnaissance mission to locate al-Qaeda training camps in eastern Afghanistan.

and coordinated a precision air campaign from their mountainous vantage points.

With most of the missions carried out under the cover of darkness, Operation Enduring Freedom was, by many accounts, the most secretive war in history. The American public was told very little of the day-to-day operations, and the news media were kept at bay. One American correspondent, however, was close enough to the action in the early stages of the war to realize that U.S.

Special Forces were operating "in a murky world where success is sometimes hard to measure and outright victory even harder to declare, where good intelligence can be difficult to come by and bad intelligence can have deadly consequences."[2]

Ultimately, in a war that relied so heavily on secret surveillance and covert attacks, the U.S.-led coalition's inability to capture or kill Osama bin Laden after a determined search was seen by some as a failure of intelligence. Others put the blame squarely on the shoulders of U.S. military planners, who opted to use fewer American ground troops in favor of the Afghan proxy force. According to military historian Stephen Tanner, that strategy in the end reflected poorly on the United States:

> It was a serious mistake, in my opinion, for America not to have used ground troops more aggressively in response to September 11. Its reliance, as in the previous decade, on stand-off missiles, high-level bombers, and other aircraft reaffirmed that the United States military cannot be fought but can only be circumvented. The success of U.S. air power and the participation of a few courageous elites in Afghanistan has perhaps made less impression on the world than the fact that given the most heinous provocation in modern times [the attacks of 9/11], the bulk of the U.S. forces hesitated to engage. The reluctance of the United States to risk military casualties—enforced during the 1990s and inexplicably continued after September 11—is a hidden drain on its authority and respect with which the world normally views a great power. This opinion could not be held without the parallel conviction that Americans, individually, are unsurpassed in courage and combat skill. The problem seems to lie in cautious command tied to political or media obsessions.[3]

Criticism of the way the campaign was conceived and carried out notwithstanding, the United States accomplished much of what it said it intended to do in Afghanistan. At the end of the major fighting, the Taliban regime was no longer in power, and the Afghan peoples were free to begin the process of rebuilding their lives and country. Perhaps more important, however, military operations left the al-Qaeda network in disarray, severely limiting the terrorists' ability to plan and carry out future attacks against the United States.

Chapter 1

Afghanistan: A Land of Chaos and Conflict

Afghanistan's snow-capped mountains and wide-open plains, fertile valleys and scorching deserts provide a great many contrasts in terrain in a country roughly the size of Texas. The Central Asian nation is completely landlocked, bordered by Turkmenistan, Uzbekistan, and Tajikistan to the north; China to the northeast; Pakistan to the east and south; and Iran to the west. Dividing north from south is the great Hindu Kush mountain range. The journey across the Hindu Kush is treacherous, possible only along a dozen or so passes.

For thousands of years, foreign armies, including those led by Alexander the Great and Genghis Khan, have traversed these mountain passes in attempts to conquer Afghanistan. The territory was valuable because of its strategic position along the historic trading routes known as the Silk Road. Control of Afghanistan often meant the control of trade between Afghanistan and Egypt, Mesopotamia (now parts of present-day Syria, Turkey, and Iraq), and beyond. Ancient

Afghanistan was also desired because it was one of the important cultural centers of its time, teeming with brilliant scholars and artists. Ruling Afghanistan often amounted to control of ideas and creativity in the region.

The Greeks, Mongols, and Persians all invaded the land at various times throughout history and claimed it as their own. Because of repeated invasions by outsiders, Afghanistan is an ethnic mosaic of Arabic, Chinese, Mongolian, Persian, and various other cultures. Each invading people brought with them customs, beliefs, and identities that in time formed a culture that is distinctly Afghan. Primarily tribal in nature, Afghan society featured a blend of sedentary and nomadic ways of life. Various ethnic groups with different languages and cultures settled in oases and fertile valleys and lived peacefully as farmers, but many others moved from place to place as nomads and seized lands in ongoing power struggles. The nomadic Hephthalites, for example, emerged from Central Asia in A.D. 400

and conquered about thirty kingdoms in the Afghan region. They held power for 165 years until their defeat at the hands of the Sassanians and western Turks.

Afghans also practiced various religions, such as Buddhism and Hinduism, but this changed when Arab armies swept into the region in the seventh century and brought with them the new religion of Islam. The Afghan people—like other peoples conquered by the Arabs—were forced to convert to Islam and worship Allah. Although the Afghans resisted for many for years, over time they became fervent believers and willing practi-

tioners of the Muslim faith. In the thirteenth century, the Mongol warlord Genghis Khan learned just how entrenched Islam had become in Afghan society. After leading his army in an invasion of Afghanistan in 1220, he attempted to erase Islam from the region by killing thousands of people and destroying entire cities. The defiant Afghans remained strong in their faith, calling for a jihad (holy struggle) against their Mongol oppressors, and by the end of the thirteenth century, Khan's own descendants had given up the fight and had themselves become firm believers in Allah.

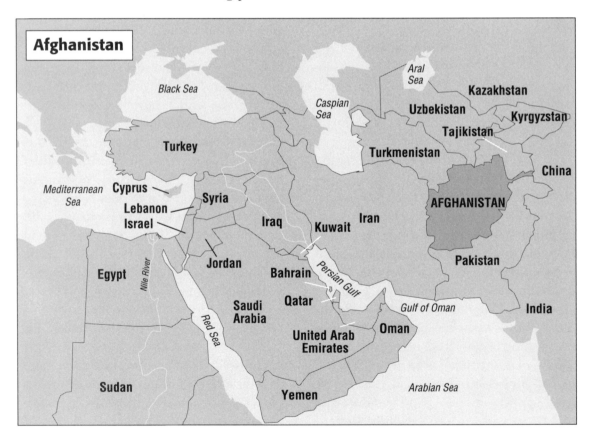

The Great Game

Six hundred years later, another invading army learned the same lesson, that outsiders attempt to control the unruly Afghan tribes at their own peril. In the nineteenth century, Afghanistan was caught between the expanding British and czarist Russian empires. The struggle between the two powers for influence over this region was dubbed by Western observers "the Great Game." According to Afghan historian Neamatollah Nojumi, the violent period shaped Afghan traditions and values:

> The historical resistance to the external aggressors during the eighteenth, nineteenth, and twentieth centuries impacted the country and its people in all aspects. For example, Afghans held tightly to their cultural values and traditions; weapons became commonplace in almost all households. Afghans were very sensitive to foreign political influence as independence and individualism were very important values in their society.[4]

The fierce independence that had come to define the Afghan tribes over the centuries showed itself during the First Anglo–Afghan War (1839–1842). The war was the result of an alliance forged by Russian leaders with Afghan emir Dost Muhammad. Fearing Russia would eventually use Afghanistan as a staging area to threaten India, Britain's colony, British and Indian troops invaded Afghanistan. They occupied Kabul, the capital city, and installed a king. But in a rare display of tribal unity, Afghan warriors mounted an attack against British and Indian forces, forcing a massive retreat from Kabul. Then in a brutal ambush, the Afghans attacked. Out of sixteen thousand fleeing British and Indian soldiers and camp followers, only one person survived. Humiliated by the defeat, the British reduced their military presence in Afghanistan yet maintained diplomatic ties over the next four decades.

Britain, however, continued to fear Russian influence over Afghanistan, and in 1878 British troops invaded once again. As before, the invaders met strong resistance from Afghan tribesmen. The campaign lasted two years, and the British again suffered heavy casualties. Eventually, however, in exchange for British support and protection, Afghan ruler Abdorrahman Khan ceded to Britain control over Afghanistan's foreign affairs and strategic border areas, including the heavily traveled Khyber Pass. In the last two decades of the nineteenth century, Britain and Russia agreed on the geographic boundaries of Afghanistan, which up to that point had not been clearly defined. Russia seized territories in the north (now Uzbekistan, Tajikistan, and Turkmenistan) while Britain carved off land in the east and the south for India. These new borders would delineate Afghanistan through the next century and beyond.

Attempts to Modernize Lead to Instability

Despite the borders having been set by foreign powers, in 1919 Abdorrahman Khan's grandson, Amanullah Khan, declared Afghanistan to be an independent nation.

Afghanistan's Diverse Ethnic Makeup

Afghanistan's tribes and ethnic groups have historically lacked a sense of national identity, in part because deep loyalties go to local leaders and tribes first and to the country second, if at all. Many tribal groups have vastly different cultures, attitudes, and languages, which has perpetuated an atmosphere of distrust and dislike for members of other ethnic groups. For centuries these tribes have fought over territory and struggled for power.

Afghanistan is a nation of nearly 28 million people, most of whom follow a traditional social system based on the family and clan. Collectively, clans make up tribes and tribes make up ethnic groups. The Pashtuns, Afghanistan's largest ethnic group, comprise 38 percent of the population. They are a proud, deeply religious, and often combative people and have long lived in the mountainous southern and eastern regions of the country, heavily concentrated along the Pakistan border. Given their majority status in Afghanistan, Pashtuns have long held a grip on leadership positions in government. The Taliban was comprised of mainly Pashtuns. The Tajiks, Afghanistan's second largest ethnic tribe with 25 percent of the population, live in northern Afghanistan, as do the nontribal Uzbeks, at 6 percent. The Hazaras and Aimaqs make up 19 percent and inhabit central and northwestern Afghanistan. The remaining 12 percent of the population is made up of minor ethnic groups who live in territorial pockets across the land.

Eventually both Britain and Russia agreed to this historic proclamation. But the Afghan people had little to celebrate. The country was faced with the daunting challenge of catching up to the industrialized world, since Abdorrahman Khan had intentionally kept Afghanistan economically unattractive in the late 1800s to deter invasion by Britain or Russia. Khan had prevented modernization by discouraging investment in factories and public works projects and limiting roads and railway construction. Nojumi notes that the decision not to modernize reinforced Afghans' tendency to isolate themselves:

Because of highly ethnic and communal diversities and because of inefficient transportation and communications systems, the linkage between governmental centers (mostly located in the towns) and rural areas was very weak. Through the course of time, this geographical and ethnic situation created a social environment that was closed to outsiders.[5]

The harshness of the terrain and climate also made it difficult for rural Afghans to develop strong connections with urban centers. During the winter, northern roads were blocked by snow, and the people of those mountainous areas learned to survive in isolation for months at a time. Moreover, almost all rural Afghans were uneducated farmers or peasants who relied on their tribal chieftains to make decisions in their communal interests. The chieftains maintained control over administrative duties regarding business, marriage, inheritance, and land disputes. Because Afghan Muslims were traditionally devout, they relied on their religious leaders to dictate not only religious practice but also social customs according to Islamic law.

Subsequent attempts to strengthen Afghanistan's central government were met with resistance. In the 1920s, Amanullah Khan began to replace the Sharia (Islamic law) with secular laws and to introduce European-inspired reforms. Among his social reforms were discouraging Afghan women from wearing veils and requiring Western dress in Kabul. Amanullah also sought to replace Afghanistan's Islam-based educational system with a primarily secular alternative, and he abolished slavery and forced labor. The Afghan ruler's efforts at reform undermined the power of both religious and tribal leaders, who sparked tribal uprisings that eventually developed into a civil war. Amanullah went into exile in 1929, and his cousin, Muhammad Nadir Shah, became the new king. Nadir Shah attempted to appease angry tribes by abolishing most of Amanullah's reforms.

While Nadir Shah regained the support of religious leaders by reinstating traditional Islamic practices in Afghan society, he also attempted a limited modernization program. Road construction projects were implemented, including the Great North Road through the Hindu Kush, making travel between urban centers and rural areas much easier. Afghanistan's economy was also strengthened with the establishment of a banking system and a long-term financial plan. In 1931, Nadir Shah also ensured national security by signing the Treaty of Neutrality and Non-Aggression with the Soviet Union. Relative calm prevailed in the country for more than ten years, but as was often the case in Afghanistan, any social progress that resulted gave way to chaos when disapproving tribes revolted in 1944 and 1945.

Cold War Battleground

Afghanistan's situation worsened four years later when a trade dispute with Pakistan nearly brought the economy to a standstill. The Soviet Union stepped in and poured millions of dollars into Afghanistan to save the fledgling nation from bankruptcy. King Muhammad Zahir Shah's prime minister and cousin, Muhammad Daoud, eventually

Soviet leaders meet with Afghanistan's prime minister (right) in 1959. The Soviet Union invested millions of dollars in Afghanistan's economy.

sought financial support from the United States as well, but his request was denied. The Cold War between the Soviet Union and the United States was in its infancy and the U.S. president, Dwight D. Eisenhower, and his advisers did not yet recognize Afghanistan's strategic significance in the struggle between the two superpowers.

The Soviets, on the other hand, willingly contributed aid to their struggling neighbor. The Soviets also built a military base at Bagram, north of Kabul, and supplied T34 tanks, MiG-17 jet fighters, helicopters, and other heavy armaments. They constructed a road connecting the Afghan capital to the Soviet Union to make the transport of military supplies easier. And in 1954 the Soviets funded the construction of a gas pipeline in northern Afghanistan. To American officials it appeared that the Soviets were well on the way to installing a Communist government in Kabul. Therefore, after initially refusing aid to Afghanistan, the United States attempted to counter the Communist threat by delivering about $150 million for the construction of roads and an international airport. The Soviets, not to be outdone, contributed $250 million. Soviet premier Nikita Khrushchev later revealed why his country was determined to outspend the United States:

It was clear to us that the Americans were penetrating Afghanistan with the obvious purpose of setting up a military base. . . . The amount of money we spent in gratuitous assistance to Afghan-

istan is a drop in the ocean compared with the price we would have had to pay in order to counter the threat of an American military base on Afghan territory. Think of the capital we would have had to lay out to finance the deployment of our own military might along our side of the Afghan border.[6]

In addition to providing financial assistance, the Soviets trained the Afghan national military. Under their guidance, it became a well-trained, well-equipped unit, which Daoud did not hesitate to use to suppress protest against his various social reforms. But his time in power came to an end in 1963, when differences with Zahir Shah led to his dismissal. Zahir Shah then began a ten-year rule over a constitutional monarchy. The Loya Jirga, the "Great National Assembly of Notables," approved a constitution in 1964, allowing political parties to form and Afghan women to vote for the first time.

The adoption of the new constitution opened the door to communism, which after a decade of Soviet influence had gained a foothold among young, progressive Afghans. In 1965, twenty-seven Afghan leftists, mostly university lecturers and civil servants, formed the pro-Communist People's Democratic Party of Afghanistan (PDPA). The PDPA was a diverse organization, however, and by 1969 the party had split into two factions: the pro-Islamic Khalq (The People) Party, led by Nur Mohammad Taraki, and the pro-Soviet Parcham (The

Banner) Party, headed by Babrak Karmal. In 1973, Parcham orchestrated a coup d'etat against Zahir Shah, the government collapsed, and Daoud returned as prime minister. Daoud shredded the constitution and thus ended Afghanistan's monarchy. He began a reign of terror by arresting, and often torturing or killing, those who opposed him, and alienated Islamic clerics by limiting religious practice under Soviet influence.

Daoud soon ran afoul of his pro-Communist PDPA supporters when in 1975 he renewed a neutrality treaty with the Soviet Union in an attempt to maintain friendly ties with both the Soviets and the Americans. In April 1978, with PDPA support, leftist army and air force commanders staged a bloody coup in which Daoud and his family were killed and Taraki was installed as head of the Democratic Republic of Afghanistan (DRA). This brief but violent period became known as the Saur (April) Revolution. For the first time, Communist officials were in power in Kabul.

Prelude to War

Taraki walked a fine line, taking orders from Moscow but, in an effort to pacify the devoutly Muslim tribes, not attempting to limit religious practice. Still, with help from the Soviets, the Afghan government soon instituted radical reforms, including abolishing marriage dowries, taking property from landowners and redistributing it to people who had no land, and making education for both sexes mandatory. The government also

Nur Mohammad Taraki speaks at a press conference after taking control of Afghanistan's government.

announced the decision to drop the tradition of invoking the name of Allah before official pronouncements. Richard and Nancy Newell explain the Afghans' reaction to the Soviet-inspired reforms:

Any one of these programs, tactlessly introduced, would almost certainly have aroused a bitter reaction among most segments of the population. When they were introduced together as a package under the red banner of communism, the effect was catastrophic. . . . Taken together, these reforms virtually guaranteed opposition. Their enforcement . . . was brought home by government servants who saw no virtue in using tact or diplomacy.[7]

Though Taraki oversaw the mass arrest, torture, and execution of his political opponents, the chaos spread, and by early 1979, twenty-four of the (then) twenty-eight Afghan provinces were in open rebellion against the government. In March of that year the Afghan military, under the command of Soviet advisers, entered Kerala, a village where people were suspected of giving support to the anti-Soviet fighters known as the mujahideen. The Afghan army rounded up more than one thousand men and boys in the village and summarily executed them when they refused to recite pro-Soviet slogans.

However, far from quelling the rebellion, this demonstration of force had the opposite effect. Many in the Afghan army who were

Afghan Refugees: The Legacy of War

The Afghan refugee crisis dates back to the mid-1970s when the nation experienced a severe and prolonged drought. Afghans who relied on farming left their homes in search of fertile land in neighboring countries. When the nation's Communist regime started a program of land redistribution in 1978, the flow of refugees increased as Afghan peasants fled the country. But the refugee situation became an international crisis when the USSR invaded Afghanistan the following year. Unleashing a wave of terror on the civilian population, the Soviets flattened entire villages, killing tens of thousands of Afghans. Many of those who survived were forced from their homes into refugee camps located in Pakistan and Iran. By the mid-1980s, the number of Afghan refugees had risen to nearly 5 million, making it the largest refugee crisis in the world. Conditions in the camps were horrendous as most Afghans went without adequate food, water, shelter, and sanitation.

Many of the refugee camps in Pakistan served a dual role: to shelter Afghans from war and to serve as bases for the mujahideen. Trained and supported by the United States and other Western nations, the mujahideen freely crossed over into Afghanistan and unleashed guerrilla attacks on the Soviet troops. Then they raced back over the border and vanished into the refugee camps. This tactic confounded the Soviets, who were often unwilling to pursue their adversaries into Pakistan. The cross-border attacks were a major factor in the Soviet decision to pull out of Afghanistan. When the last Soviet troops left in 1989, refugees remained in the camps, fearful of the Communist Najibullah regime that remained in place. Not until Najibullah fell from power in 1992 did large numbers of refugees return to Afghanistan. But the refugee camps swelled to critical levels during the civil war and the subsequent Taliban takeover of government in 1996. The Afghan refugee camps again reached critical levels before U.S. military strikes on Afghanistan in response to the attacks of September 11. When the Taliban were driven from power in December 2001, many Afghan refugees returned to their homes for the first time in years.

revolted by the killing of their own countrymen began defecting to the mujahideen. Though lightly armed, the mujahideen were trained in guerrilla tactics and launched sudden, and often shocking, attacks against the enemy. In late 1979, for example, they tortured and killed Soviet advisers and their families staying in Herat. The DRA military troops quashed that uprising, killing up to twenty thousand Afghans in the process. The massacre provoked more Afghan military defections, an unwelcome development for Soviet officials already concerned that control was slipping away in Afghanistan. Ralph H. Magnus and Eden Naby explain:

The situation had shifted dramatically against the Soviet Union. Instead of exploiting a compliant regional ally under a Marxist regime to help advance its interests, [Soviet leader] Brezhnev faced a situation fast approaching chaos. The new regime's cadres, few enough to begin with, were divided into hostile factions in the process of busily trying to murder one another. More important, the resistance of the Afghan people, based on national, social, and religious grounds, was increasingly successful in challenging the authority of the PDPA regime in the provinces.[8]

Soviet Invasion and the Mujahideen Resistance

Soviet interests were further threatened when, in October 1979, Taraki was over-thrown and then assassinated. This angered Soviet leaders, who preferred Taraki over his successor, Hafizullah Amin. Two months later they launched a full-scale invasion of Afghanistan. The Red Army moved in rapidly, killed Amin, and installed a puppet regime headed by Babrak Karmal. Soviet-DRA forces immediately set out to end all remaining opposition with brutal force. Large areas of the country were targeted with chemical weapons, killing livestock and crops in the process. International condemnation was swift, but it did little to stop the Soviets from their assault. In less than one week they controlled major Afghan cities and government.

In response to the attack on their people, Afghanistan's religious leaders called for a jihad against the Soviets, and thousands of Muslims from throughout the Middle East and Central Asia joined the resistance. These recruits traveled to Pakistan and Saudi Arabia, where they received training in guerrilla warfare from Pakistani, Saudi, and American intelligence agents. These new fighters then slipped into Afghanistan to join the battle against the Soviets. According to journalist Ahmed Rashid,

This was part of a wider U.S., Pakistani, and Saudi plan to recruit radical Muslims from around the world to fight with the Afghans. Between 1982 and 1992 thirty-five thousand Muslim radicals from forty-three Islamic countries fought for the [mujahideen]. Tens of thousands more studied in the thousands of new

Soviet soldiers keep watch for mujahideen fighters. Soviet forces invaded Afghanistan in 1979, beginning a war that lasted ten years.

government-funded madrassahs [religious schools] in Pakistan. Eventually more than a hundred thousand Muslim radicals from around the world had direct contact with Pakistan and Afghanistan.[9]

For the next ten years the Soviet Red Army tried to consolidate its control of the country. The effort was disastrous for both Afghans and Soviets. As losses among its ground troops mounted, the Red Army shifted to an air war. Using bombers, fighters, attack helicopters, and gunships, the Soviets began a massive depopulation campaign, killing hundreds of thousands of civilians and forcing mil-lions of others into refugee camps in Pakistan and Iran. But the Soviets also suffered heavy casualties, especially after operatives from the U.S. Central Intelligence Agency (CIA) began smuggling surface-to-air Stinger missiles to mujahideen forces. The Stingers, which could be fired by one or two fighters, were highly effective against Soviet warplanes. By downing their aircraft and making travel by land extremely dangerous, the mujahideen fought the Russians to a virtual standstill.

Civil War Leads to the Rise of the Taliban

In the Soviet Union the growing casualties led to vocal opposition to the war, and in 1989 Mikhail Gorbachev, who had become the Soviet leader in 1985, pulled his nation's troops out of Afghanistan. The end to fighting was little comfort to Afghans, though. They were left with a country filled with land mines and unexploded bombs. Cities were in rubble, and economic, political, and social institutions—fragile before the invasion—were in shambles. Mohammad Najibullah replaced Karmal as leader but could not restore stability to the country. The United States and most other Western nations that had aided the Afghan resistance during the war withdrew their support, leaving the devastated nation to its own devices.

The Soviets, in their haste to withdraw, also left behind large numbers of weapons, contributing to the nation's instability.

Shortly after the Soviet pullout, fighting broke out between the mujahideen and government militias. The mujahideen won that fight but eventually turned their guns on one another. Central Asian scholar Martin McCauley notes that the civil and ethnic conflict settled nothing and, in fact, set the stage for further unrest:

> Given Afghan history, it was absolutely inevitable that the various [mujahideen] groups would fall out and begin fighting one another for supremacy. They laid the country waste as a result. President Najibullah, who had held power since the Soviets departed, fell into the hands of the [mujahideen]. . . . For the first time in 300 years the Pashtuns were not in control of Kabul. It had been captured by Tajiks, under the command of Ahmed Shah Masoud, and the Uzbek general, Rashid Dostum. The new government was heavily influenced by Tajiks and this

Mullah Mohammad Omar: Reclusive Leader

Mullah Mohammad Omar led the hard-line Islamic Taliban, a radical group that emerged from Pakistan in the mid-1990s in an effort to defeat the mujahideen warlords in the civil war ravaging Afghanistan. Known as "Commander of the Faithful," he swiftly rose to power following an incident in which he removed a rarely seen cloth said to have been worn by the Prophet Muhammad from Kandahar's grand mosque and waved it from the rooftop to rally followers below. Taliban foot soldiers then went on to conquer Kabul, and Mullah Omar remained their figurehead. He cultivated a mysterious image: No Western journalist has ever met him, and only one photograph of him is said to exist. The reclusive figure has one eye stitched shut, the result of a wound he sustained during a gunfight with Soviet troops. It was during the war with the Soviets that Mullah Omar and Osama bin Laden became friends. The two men have other ties as well. Mullah Omar is thought to be married to bin Laden's oldest daughter, and bin Laden is believed to have taken one of Mullah Omar's daughters as his fourth wife.

infuriated the Pashtuns. They wanted to attack Kabul in order to regain control of the capital.[10]

The Tajiks were not destined to remain in charge for long. In 1994 a group of militant Pashtuns, called the Taliban, emerged from Islamic schools in Pakistan known as madrassas and began settling in southern Afghanistan. Led by the reclusive Mullah Mohammad Omar, the Taliban was a fierce, fanatically religious group that followed a narrow interpretation of Islam. Supplied with weapons and training from Pakistani Inter-Service Intelligence (ISI), the Taliban defeated the mujahideen warlord, Gulbuddin Hekmatyar, to capture Kandahār and Charasiab. The mujahideen retreated to the north, where they regrouped and joined forces with other warlords' troops under the name Northern Alliance. The Taliban, however, continued to push northward, and in September 1996 captured Kabul from Massoud. The Taliban found a warm welcome in Afghanistan, as one British Broadcasting Corporation (BBC) reporter noted:

> Ordinary Afghans, weary of the prevailing lawlessness in many parts of the country, were often delighted by [Taliban] successes in stamping out corruption, restoring peace and allowing commerce to flourish again. Their refusal to deal with the existing warlords whose rivalries had caused so much killing and destruction also earned them respect.[11]

Taliban Extremism and the Threat to America

Once in power the Taliban began establishing what they considered a pure Islamic state. In keeping with a strict interpretation of the Koran, men were required to grow beards and women were denied schooling and health care. The Taliban also believed television and music were frivolous and inherently anti-Islamic and therefore banned both forms of entertainment. Afghans unhappy with the strict lifestyle imposed upon them soon learned to keep quiet. Those who did speak out were often publicly beaten or even executed. The Taliban were just as harsh toward fellow Muslims whose beliefs differed slightly from their own. The Taliban, who were of the Sunni branch of Islam, were particularly cruel to one ethnic group, the Hazaras, who were members of the other major branch of Islam, Shia. Scholar M.J. Gohari tells the story:

> On August 8, 1998, and the days that followed, the Taliban militiamen and their allies including militant Muslims from neighboring Pakistan systematically executed between 2,000 and 5,000 civilians in one of the deadliest mass killings of civilians in two decades of warfare in Afghanistan. According to some reports the Taliban militiamen searched house to house for males of fighting age who belonged to the Hazara ethnic minority. Hazaras were gunned down in front of their families or had their throats cut. Others, thrown into the city's over-

crowded jail, were executed by firing squads or loaded into tractor-trailers, where they sweltered all day in the summer sun, with doors shut, until most perished from suffocation or heat stroke.[12]

The United States took notice of the events occurring in Afghanistan. But most alarming to American officials was Mullah Omar's friendship with a known terrorist, Saudi-born Osama bin Laden. Both Mullah Omar and bin Laden were outspoken critics of U.S. foreign policy in the Middle East. The men made no secret of their hatred of Israel, which they said was illegally occupying the Palestinian people's land. They asserted that U.S. financial and military support of the Jewish state made America an enemy of the Muslim world. The two men also objected to U.S. troops that had been stationed in Saudi Arabia since the Persian Gulf War ended in 1991. To Mullah Omar and bin Laden, the United States had become the new infidel and had to be attacked—both overseas and on U.S. soil.

Chapter 2

Osama bin Laden and al-Qaeda Terror Network

Until the morning of September 11, 2001, few Americans had heard of Osama bin Laden. Although he was known to have orchestrated spectacular terrorist attacks on U.S. interests, few Americans had been killed or hurt in those. Then, in the space of a few horrifying minutes, Osama bin Laden became America's most wanted criminal.

Little in Osama bin Laden's early years pointed to his developing into a terrorist mastermind. He was born in 1957 in Riyadh, Saudi Arabia, the seventeenth of fifty-one children fathered by Muhammad bin Laden, a man of Yemeni descent. Osama bin Laden's mother, Hamida, was a daughter of a Syrian trader. Muhammad bin Laden was the founder of the Bin Laden Group, a construction company that prospered by building palaces for the Saudi royal family. Bin Laden's company also won contracts for the construction of the Medina-Jedda highway and for the renovation of mosques in the holy cities of Mecca and Medina. Muhammad bin Laden, who was a member of one of the most conservative branches of Sunni Islam, was generous with his wealth and diligently followed the Islamic practice of almsgiving. He rarely left home without a pocketful of money to dole out to the poor.

Muhammad bin Laden insisted that his children observe strict religious and social codes. However, although Osama expressed interest in Islam, he showed no overt signs of religious fanaticism early in life. He attended an elite, Western-style school in Jedda and learned to speak English. According to Brian Fyfield-Shayler, his teacher in Jedda, Osama "was very courteous—more so than any of the others in his class. Physically, he was outstanding because he was taller, more handsome and fairer than most of the other boys. He also stood out as he was singularly gracious and polite, and had a great deal of inner confidence."[13]

In 1974 Osama bin Laden, following his family's wishes, entered King Abdul Aziz University in Jedda to study civil engineering in the expectation that he would one day lead the family business. But Osama bin Laden had by this time begun to show a religious bent, and he eventually became fascinated with the teachings of a radical Islamic academician, Abdallah Azzam, as reporter Jason Burke explains:

Osama bin Laden studied at a Western-style school and a Saudi Arabian university before becoming fascinated with radical Islamic teachings.

Azzam's recorded sermons . . . brilliantly caught the mood of many disaffected young Muslims. Jedda itself—and King Abdul Aziz University—was a center for Islamic dissidents from all over the Muslim world. In its mosques and [medrassas] they preached a severe message: only an absolute return to the values of conservative Islam could protect the Muslim world from the dangers and decadence of the West.[14]

Azzam, founder of the Palestinian guerrilla group known as Hamas, often mixed politics and religion in his messages, and he spoke out sharply against Israel and the United States for what he believed was unfair treatment of the Palestinians. According to Azzam and many other radicals of the day, Israel was an illegitimate state whose people were occupying the Palestinian homeland, and the American government made this occupation possible through its military and financial support. Bin Laden was transformed by Azzam's words and developed a deep distrust of the United States.

Seeds of Radical Islam Take Root

Although Azzam's influence on bin Laden was profound, several regional events affected him just as profoundly. In February 1979 an Islamic revolution in Iran forced the removal of Shah Mohammad Reza Pahlavi, considered by most Muslims to be a puppet of the United States. The shah was replaced by a conservative Islamic cleric, Ayatollah Khomeini. By then bin Laden had become a vocal critic of the United States, and he supported any anti-American cause. Later that year a group of Islamic extremists, armed with guns, stormed the grand mosque at Mecca in protest of the Saudi royal family, and they demanded a national return to fundamental Islam. Saudi and French security forces eventually overtook the extremists in a bloody gunfight, but bin Laden drew inspiration from the rebels. He considered the men true Muslims because they were willing to take a stand for their religion, and he wanted to be more like them. When the Soviet army invaded Afghanistan one month later, he had found a cause that would not only strengthen his radical beliefs but allow him to aid the defense of Islam from the Communist infidels. The twenty-three-year-old traveled to Peshawar, Pakistan, to offer his support. "That trip which was [a] secret trip lasted for almost a month and was an exploratory rather than [an] action trip," said a source close to bin Laden:

> He went back to the kingdom [Saudi Arabia] and started lobbying with his brothers, relatives and friends at the school to support the [mujahideen]. He succeeded in collecting [a] huge amount of money and material as donations to [the] jihad. He made another trip to take this material. He took with him [a] few Pakistanis and Afghanis who were working in [the] bin Laden company. . . . Again, he did not stay more than a month. The trip was to Pakistan and the border only and was not to Afghanistan. He went on collecting

money and going in short trips once or twice a year until 1982.[15]

During his initial trip to Peshawar, bin Laden met Abdallah Azzam, who had so impressed him at King Abdul Aziz University. Azzam and bin Laden established a worldwide network called Mekhtab al Khidemat (MaK) to recruit Muslims for the resistance to the Soviet occupation. The two men set up recruiting centers in fifty countries around the world, including Egypt, Pakistan, Saudi Arabia, and the United States. Enlisting thousands of volunteers for MaK, Azzam and bin Laden sheltered and transported them to the battlefield. Azzam and bin Laden also created paramilitary training camps in Afghanistan and Pakistan, where more than ten thousand radical Muslims trained for combat. Most of the men were from Saudi Arabia, but many others came from Algeria, Pakistan, Sudan, and Yemen.

Bin Laden Joins the Fight

By the early 1980s bin Laden was not just radical; he was rich enough to support radical Islamic causes in a material way. Bin Laden's father had died in 1968 and left him some $80 million. That sum had grown to more than $250 million as a result of overseas investments. Osama bin Laden's wealth gave him both power and prestige in Afghanistan, and like his father he gave generously. He visited wounded mujahideen fighters at medical clinics and comforted them with religious words of praise and simple treats. Before leaving he presented each soldier's

Mujahideen rebels rest in the mountains of eastern Afghanistan. Osama bin Laden provided financial support to the mujahideen.

family with a large gift of money to show his appreciation. Many recipients were drawn to bin Laden emotionally and swore their allegiance to him.

The wealthy Saudi's fame grew when reports of his aid to the Afghan resistance began appearing in Middle Eastern newspapers. Word of his generosity inspired thousands of Arab men to join the strug-

gle against the Soviets. To accommodate the recruits entering Peshawar, bin Laden and Azzam rented a house where the new arrivals could stay while they trained. The volunteers received combat training and religious instruction at what bin Laden called Beit-al-Ansar (House of the Faithful). They were then transferred to the battlefield where they joined the mujahideen in the struggle against the Soviets.

Bin Laden's role in the Afghan resistance effort continued to expand as he began undertaking large construction projects inside Afghanistan in support of the war. Rohan Gunaratna, an expert on Middle Eastern affairs explains:

By the mid-1980s Osama was drawing on his family skills, importing heavy machinery, building roads and cave complexes, and supervising the blasting of massive tunnels into the Zazi mountains of Paktia which were to hide field hospitals and arms depots. These facilities, spanning several kilometers, provided for the training and accommodation of hundreds of fighters.[16]

Eventually bin Laden decided he was ready to challenge the Soviets directly and entered Afghanistan to join the fight. Within two years he had built six training camps inside the country to train his own fighting force. Bin Laden enlisted veterans from Syria and Egypt and began conducting operations against the Soviets. In one battle bin Laden and fifty fighters under his command, armed with only rifles and rocket launchers, withstood a major assault by the Red Army. This exploit solidified bin Laden's image in the Muslim world as a hero of legendary proportions. In a 1993 interview with journalist Robert Fisk, bin Laden spoke of the reasons for his bravery on the battlefield:

No, I was never afraid of death. As Muslims, we believe that when we die, we go to heaven. Before a battle, God sends us seqina, tranquillity. Once I was only thirty metres away from the Russians and they were trying to capture me. I was under bombardment, but I was so peaceful in my heart that I fell asleep. This experience has been written about in our earliest books. I saw a 120-mm mortar shell land in front of me, but it did not blow up. Four more bombs were dropped from a Russian plane on our headquarters but they did not explode.[17]

The Birth of al-Qaeda

Official tracking of enlistments and casualties in the largely guerrilla-style mujahideen forces was sketchy. Bin Laden's renown was such that in the late 1980s the parents and wives of missing mujahideen began contacting him for help in finding their loved ones. Knowing he had no means of retracing the fighters' movements, in 1988 bin Laden and a close associate named Muhammad Atef set up a network to locate missing fighters and to keep better track of those who entered the battlefield to participate in the resistance. This organization, called al-Qaeda, had been in operation only one year when the Soviets announced their pullout of Afghanistan. Bin Laden's organization remained in Peshawar, however, to funnel aid to the mujahideen fighting the Communist regime still in place in Afghanistan. But the al-Qaeda leader eventually advised many of the men to return home to prepare for holy wars in their own countries. According to author John Barry, however, bin Laden was not the only one responsible for turning the Arab and Afghan mujahideen into dangerous Islamic extremists:

[The United States] turned those who fought the Soviets into heroes and encouraged religious young Arabs to take up arms against the ungodly. The plan succeeded all too well. By the time Soviet troops left Afghanistan in 1989, a cohort of bloodied, well-armed, Islamic soldiers were ready to be unleashed, like some medieval plague, on an unsuspecting world. It is out of that group—the Arab Afghans—that the terrorist cadres of the world have been drawn. And by the end of the Afghan war, bin Laden was ready to become the leader of many of them.[18]

Bin Laden followed his own advice and returned to Saudia Arabia. He assumed an active role in his family's construction business in Jedda, though he remained in frequent contact with al-Qaeda and found time to give speeches in the region about the success of the Afghan resistance. In his speeches he warned of an imminent invasion of Kuwait and Saudi Arabia by Iraqi leader Saddam Hussein to take control of the two nations' oil fields. The Saudi regime, which wanted to avoid antagonizing the volatile Iraqi leader, instructed bin Laden to stop giving speeches and confined him to Jedda.

Bin Laden's prophecies seemed to be borne out when, in 1991, Hussein ordered a military invasion of Kuwait. The Iraqi army quickly seized the tiny nation's oil fields and seemed poised to move against Saudi Arabia next. Bin Laden responded to the threat by calling for a jihad against Iraq. According to Gunaratna, bin Laden opposed the Saudi government's proposal to defend the nation against a possible Iraqi invasion with U.S. help:

As the Saudi royal family discussed inviting US troops to repel the Iraqis and establish a presence in their country, Osama approached them with an alternative plan, namely to offer his services to forge an anti–Saddam Hussein coalition by enlisting 5,000 mujahideen veterans who were still in Afghanistan. His proposal was rejected, US [and European] troops were invited into the Holy Kingdom, and Osama was humiliated. . . . The US launched Operation Desert Shield by dispatching paratroopers, an armoured brigade, and jet fighters to Saudi Arabia on August 7. Osama detested the very idea of armed non-Muslims even entering the land of the two holy mosques, and expressed his displeasure.[19]

Bin Laden considered the United States an infidel both because it was a predominantly Christian nation and because it strongly supported Israel. Basing U.S. troops on land sacred to Muslims therefore enraged him. He lobbied for and received a fatwa, or legal decree, from Islamic scholars that said training and readiness to fight a holy war against the United States was every Muslim's religious duty. He circulated the fatwa and encouraged people to go to Afghanistan and train for what he considered to be an impending jihad.

Al-Qaeda Goes on the Attack

The Saudi government had promised that U.S. forces would leave the kingdom after Iraq's defeat, but at the conclusion of the Gulf War, the regime allowed U.S. forces to remain in the country. Bin Laden harshly criticized this decision, calling King Fahd a false Muslim and an instrument of the U.S. government, and he encouraged Arab Mus-

U.S. armored vehicles move across Saudi Arabia during the Gulf War. The presence of U.S. forces in Saudi Arabia angered bin Laden.

1993 World Trade Center Bombing

The attacks that destroyed the World Trade Center on September 11, 2001, were not the first attempt against the famous landmark. On February 26, 1993, four men placed a massive bomb in the parking garage beneath the north tower of the World Trade Center. The attempt of the terrorists was to topple both towers and kill the many thousands of workers inside. The blast shook the structure and left a crater beneath more than three stories deep, but the tower stood. Cyanide gas released from the bomb killed six people and injured more than one thousand others. Fortunately, heat from the explosion broke down the gas, or the death toll could have been much higher.

The mastermind behind the attack, Ramzi Ahmed Yousef, was captured two years later in Pakistan. He was then extradited to the United States, tried in court, and sentenced to life in prison. Yousef had earlier attended an al-Qaeda training camp in Afghanistan, where he was taught the methods of bomb making. Authorities believe that Yousef had contact with Osama bin Laden and that the terrorist leader may even have funded this, the first terrorist attempt against the World Trade Center.

lims to rise up against the Saudi ruler. In 1992 the Saudis responded to bin Laden's verbal attacks by forcing him out of the country, leaving him without a homeland. He went to Pakistan first and then to Afghanistan, but he was still considered such a threat that Saudi and Pakistani intelligence agencies tried several times to assassinate him. He managed to escape death each time when friends in both organizations tipped him off.

Fearing additional attempts on his life, bin Laden moved to Sudan. There, a political party known as the National Islamic Front (NIF) was in power, and its leader, the fiercely anti-American Hassun al Turabi, was a friend of bin Laden's from the Afghan war. Bin Laden settled in the capital city of Khartoum and set up a road construction company, two large farms, and a tannery. He hired nearly five hundred former mujahideen and put them to work, mainly building roads. Three al-Qaeda members, Muhammad Atef, Saif Al-Adel, and Abdullah Ahmed Abdullah, ac-companied him to Sudan and assumed top-level positions in al-Qaeda, which by then had become a complex organization, with a consultation council, military committee, and religious/fatwa committee.

With U.S. troops still in Saudi Arabia in late 1992, bin Laden and his fellow al-Qaeda members actively plotted ways to strike Americans wherever they could in the region. He began working with Sudan's NIF to acquire biological, chemical, and nuclear weapons. The CIA, at the time, believed bin Laden had purchased uranium and hired an Egyptian scientist to develop a nuclear bomb. The attempt ultimately failed, but he continued searching for a way to make or acquire such weapons.

In the meantime, al-Qaeda and other terrorist groups in Khartoum began planning guerrilla-style attacks against American troops. In December 1992 al-Qaeda launched its first attack by detonating a bomb in a Yemen hotel where U.S. troops were staying. The soldiers had already left, but two Austrian tourists died in the attack. In early October 1993 al-Qaeda assisted Somalis in shooting down two U.S. Black Hawk helicopters in Mogadishu, Somalia. In the gun battle that followed, eighteen U.S. soldiers died. Americans were shocked and infuriated when they saw television images of Somalis dragging one of the dead pilots through the streets. In 1995 terrorists with links to al-Qaeda set off a car bomb in Riyadh, Saudi Arabia, killing five U.S. servicemen. President Bill Clinton signed a top-secret order authorizing the CIA to use any means necessary to destroy bin Laden's terrorist network.

Declaring War Against America

The U.S. government chose not to respond militarily to the ambush of its troops in Somalia because American citizens were not in favor of participating in an operation that seemed to resemble the Vietnam War, in which U.S. troops had struggled for years without defeating their enemy. The incident did, however, result in American officials putting intense pressure on the Sudanese government to capture bin Laden and turn him over to them. With Sudan no longer a safe haven, bin Laden returned to Afghanistan in May 1996. He was soon reunited with his friend Mullah Omar, whose Taliban followers were closing in on Kabul. Bin Laden contributed millions of dollars to the Taliban regime as it strove to create a pure Islamic state. In return he was given permission to establish camps where al-Qaeda could train men to carry out more terrorist mis-

sions. On August 23, 1996, in a letter issued from his base in the Hindu Kush mountains in Khurasan, Afghanistan, bin Laden essentially declared war against Israel and the United States. Bin Laden's letter read in part,

> My Muslim brothers: your brothers in Palestine and in the land of the two Holy Places [i.e., Saudi Arabia] are calling upon your help and asking you to take part in fighting against the enemy—the Americans and the Israelis. They are asking you to do whatever you can to expel the enemies out of the sanctities of Islam.[20]

Two years later, the al-Qaeda leader went even further. After meeting with representatives of several terrorist groups, bin Laden, who by then believed he had the authority to issue his own fatwas, issued one entitled "Jihad Against Jews and Crusaders," in which he wrote that it was an individual duty for every Muslim to kill Americans and their allies, even civilians.

Well hidden in Afghanistan, bin Laden continued planning attacks on American interests. In August, on the eight-year anniversary of the ordering of U.S. troops into Saudi Arabia, two al-Qaeda cells simultaneously detonated bombs at U.S. embassies in Kenya and Tanzania. Twelve Americans and more than two hundred others were killed in the attacks. In retaliation, two weeks later Clinton ordered cruise missile strikes against six al-Qaeda training camps in eastern

Afghanistan and a pharmaceutical plant in the Sudanese capital, Khartoum, where U.S. officials believed bin Laden was developing chemical weapons. The strikes killed twenty-six people, but bin Laden was not among them. Not only did the American response fail to kill bin Laden, it failed to deter him from his mission. CIA director George Tenet told listeners during a Senate meeting that "there is not the slightest doubt that Osama bin Laden, his worldwide allies and his sympathizers are planning further attacks against us."[21]

Bin Laden, at this point, remained safely hidden from the CIA operatives and U.S. Special Forces intelligence officers who were tracking him inside Afghanistan. But in December 1998 bin Laden allowed ABC News to broadcast an interview with him from inside his mountainous Afghan sanctuary. Most Americans were unfamiliar with bin Laden at the time, but they quickly

Rescue workers comb through the rubble of the U.S. embassy in Kenya in the aftermath of the 1998 bombing.

took notice when he used the interview to further raise the threat level against the United States, saying:

> We [al-Qaeda] say to the Americans as people and to American mothers, if they cherish their lives and if they cherish their sons, they must elect an American patriotic government that caters to their interests not the interests of the Jews. If the present injustice continues with the wave of national consciousness, it will inevitably move the battle to American soil. . . . This is my message to the American people.[22]

The United States took bin Laden's threat seriously, and in 1999 the CIA began training sixty Pakistani commandos for a covert operation to capture the terrorist leader. But a coup in Pakistan that upended that nation's government effectively ended the plan. The CIA then considered other ways to snare bin Laden. One of the options

the Clinton administration was considering at the time was a nighttime assault on the al-Qaeda leader's camp. The mission was to be carried out by U.S. Special Forces flown into position by helicopters, but it was eventually abandoned because such a raid would have to be carried out in darkness, making the risk of deadly midair collisions unacceptably high.

Left to continue operations largely undisturbed, by 2000 al-Qaeda was a worldwide network with terrorist cells in more than twenty countries, waiting for the word from bin Laden to attack. Yet al-Qaeda continued to expand. The next year bin Laden's organization officially joined forces with Ayman al-Zawahiri's Egyptian Islamic Jihad, which had taken the leading role in carrying out a devastating suicide attack against the USS *Cole*, docked in Yemen in October 2000. The bombing killed seventeen U.S. sailors and nearly sank the navy destroyer. Together, al-Qaeda and Egyptian Islamic Jihad formed a sophisticated network that was becoming more specialized in making

Bin Laden's Fatwa Targets Americans

Between August 1996 and February 1998, Osama bin Laden issued two fatwas in which he condemned the United States for its continued military presence in Saudi Arabia following the Persian Gulf War of 1991. U.S. intelligence officials had been well aware of the potential threat he represented to the country. It was the second fatwa, however, that alarmed President Bill Clinton and others in Washington. In this decree, bin Laden first urged the killing of Americans, including civilians. The U.S. government took the

threat seriously and offered a $5 million reward for his capture, while the FBI eventually put him at the top of their most-wanted list. In late 1998 the government indicted bin Laden for the conspiracy to kill U.S. nationals through various overseas attacks in the 1990s and for the embassy bombings in Kenya and Tanzania earlier in 1998. But bin Laden had found safe haven under the Taliban regime in Afghanistan and remained well hidden, safely outside the reach of the United States.

bombs and planning for large-scale terrorist operations against Western nations.

America Under Attack

Even before formally joining forces, al-Qaeda and Egyptian Islamic Jihad had begun working together on their most audacious act yet—a massive attack inside the United States, one that would make good on bin Laden's threat to bring terrorism to American soil. Beginning in early 2000, nineteen al-Qaeda terrorists entered the United States to begin training, although they knew little about the mission they were to carry out. They were instructed to blend into American society. They shaved their beards and stayed away from mosques to avoid suspicion. Some of the men were also told to enroll in aviation schools and learn to fly jetliners.

During the week of September 6, 2001, the nineteen al-Qaeda operatives traveled in four groups to Boston, Massachusetts; Portland, Maine; Newark, New Jersey; and Washington, D.C. They all carried identical copies of an anonymous letter that U.S. authorities would later find. Written in Arabic, the letter read in part:

> Purify your heart and forget something called life, for the time of play is gone and the time of truth has come. . . . When the plane starts moving, then you are traveling toward God and what a blessing that travel is.[23]

On the morning of September 11, after finally learning the full scope of their mission, the nineteen men boarded four different airliners in three separate cities: American Airlines Flight 11 and United Airlines Flight 175 in Boston; American Flight 77 in Washington; and United Flight 93 in Newark. Once the planes were in the air, the terrorists used box cutters they were carrying to overpower the crew and seize the cockpit. Flight controllers knew something ominous was unfolding when all four planes' tracking signals stopped. At 8:46 A.M., American Flight 11, piloted by Ustad Mohammed Atta, roared low across New York City and slammed into the 110-story north tower of the World Trade Center, causing a horrific explosion. Sixteen minutes later United Flight 175 swept in and struck the south tower, creating another huge fireball. If there was any question that terrorists were involved in the first crash, it was confirmed upon the second direct hit. To people watching the horrifying scenes on television or from the streets of New York below, America was clearly under attack.

At 9:37 A.M., American Flight 77 streaked low across the Washington skyline and crashed into the Pentagon. Meanwhile, United Flight 93 made a sharp bank over Cleveland, Ohio, and was on a direct course for Washington, D.C. Authorities would later conclude it was bound for either the White House or the U.S. Capitol, but passengers stormed the cockpit and attempted to wrest the plane's controls from the hijackers. The jetliner crashed into a field in southwestern Pennsylvania at 10:10 A.M.

The scene in New York City was one of complete pandemonium as flames and

Al-Qaeda's High Command

At the time of the terrorist attacks on September 11, the al-Qaeda network was made up of men from various nations and included several different terrorist organizations, yet its command-and-control structure was well defined. Osama bin Laden was clearly at the top, with Ayman al-Zawahiri, a trained surgeon from Egypt, second in command. Al-Zawahiri, who formerly led the Egyptian Islamic Jihad terrorist organization, worked with bin Laden for several years and was responsible for articulating the network's ideology in pamphlets and books. Israeli intelligence has called him the "operational brains" of al-Qaeda, and he is believed to have played an active role in planning the terrorist attacks on the United States. Khalid Sheik Mohammed is thought to have been third in command as bin Laden's chief of operations and was the alleged mastermind behind the terrorist attacks in New York and Washington. U.S. officials also believe he ordered the attack on the USS *Cole* in 2000. Muhammad

Atef, who served as al-Qaeda's military commander, also assumed a large role in planning the attacks of September 11. And Abu Zubaydah, a Palestinian born in Saudi Arabia, had been placed in charge of operations at Afghanistan's training camps and is believed to have been a key recruiter in the network.

Since the war on terrorism began in October 2001, al-Qaeda's high command has undergone a radical shake-up. Atef was killed in a U.S. bombing raid in November 2001, causing Zubaydah to move up in the organization's hierarchy. But Zubaydah was captured in Pakistan in March 2002. One year later, Pakistan was the site of another high-profile arrest of an al-Qaeda lieutenant. Sheik Mohammed was apprehended there outside Islamabad in a joint U.S.-Pakistan intelligence operation. Al-Qaeda's two highest-ranking members—bin Laden and al-Zawahiri—remain at large. They are positioned firmly at the top of the FBI's most-wanted terrorists in the world.

thick black smoke poured out of the towers. With escape routes closed off from the crash, desperate workers trapped on the floors above the inferno began leaping to their deaths, adding to the horror of that day. It would soon get much worse, however. As hundreds of firefighters raced up the stairs to battle the flames, the buildings' steel framework, weakened by the intense heat from the burning jet fuel, gave way. As mil-

lions watched on television, both skyscrapers buckled under their own weight and crashed to the ground. More than three thousand people inside were killed, making this the worst attack ever on U.S. soil—larger than the Japanese attack on Pearl Harbor in 1941 that brought the United States into World War II. With those deaths, September 11, 2001, would come to be called America's darkest day.

Chapter 3

The United States Mobilizes for War

n the aftermath of the attacks on New York City and Washington, D.C., it was soon apparent that the United States would respond militarily. But the first war of the twenty-first century—what came to be called the war against terrorism—promised to be a monumental struggle, and it required America's traditional and non-traditional allies to join in the fight. Success or failure would have lasting implications, and the question became, would Americans once again enjoy the freedoms and security they had known before September 11, or would they have to learn to live in fear of similar terrorist attacks in the future?

A Defiant President

On the morning of September 11, President George W. Bush was in a Sarasota, Florida, classroom meeting with students and teachers and using the occasion to promote his proposed education reforms. At approximately 9:05 A.M., Bush's chief of staff, Andy Card, told him that airplanes had struck the World Trade Center and that America was under attack. The president quickly met with adviser Karl Rove, who recalls the president's early response:

As he walked in the room they were playing the footage of the second plane flying into the World Trade Center and he looked at the television set and said, "We're at war, get me the director of the FBI, get me the vice president."[24]

Bush was quickly ferried away by *Air Force One*, eventually landing at Offutt Air Force Base in Nebraska, where he met with members of the National Security Council. George Tenet, the CIA chief, stated with near certainty that Osama bin Laden was responsible for the events of that day. The CIA, he reported, had intercepted cell phone conversations in which al-Qaeda operatives congratulated one another after the attacks. By 6:30 P.M., Bush was back in the Oval Office preparing a speech to the nation. At 8:30 P.M., the president addressed the nation with these somber words:

Today, our fellow citizens, our way of life, our very freedom came under attack in a series of deliberate and deadly terrorist acts. The victims were in airplanes, or in their offices; secretaries, businessmen and women, military and federal workers; moms and dads, friends and neighbors. Thousands of lives were suddenly ended by evil, despicable acts of terror. . . . These acts of mass murder were intended to frighten our nation into chaos and retreat. But they have failed; our country is strong. . . . Our military is powerful, and it's prepared. . . . The search is underway for those who are behind these evil acts. I've directed the full resources of our intelligence and law enforcement communities to find those responsible and to bring them to justice.

We will make no distinction between the terrorists who committed these acts and those who harbor them.[25]

America in Shock

The attacks of September 11 had accomplished precisely what the terrorists had intended: The United States was paralyzed as many Americans were gripped by fear, uncertain of whether more attacks were to follow. Office buildings, shopping malls, and other public buildings across the nation remained closed for several days. In an unprecedented move, all flights in and out of U.S. airports were grounded, leaving travelers temporarily stranded. Americans gathered in public settings and held candlelight vigils in honor of the dead and missing.

A Presidency Transformed

In the 2000 presidential election, Republican George W. Bush was elected by the narrowest margin in U.S. history. The race between Bush and Democrat Al Gore was so close that Bush lost the popular vote but ended up winning the presidency when he received the necessary electoral college votes after controversial vote-counting was stopped in Florida. In the months after Bush's victory, Democratic critics questioned the legitimacy of his presidency and argued that his narrow election to office did not provide him a mandate in which to push his agenda through Congress.

After September 11, 2001, however, America's perception of Bush changed dramatically. Americans who were uncertain of how he would respond in a time of national tragedy soon witnessed a commander in chief rising to the challenge. His brief but powerful speech rallied firefighters and rescue workers at the World Trade Center three days after the attacks and won him praise even from the Democrats. Bush's public approval rating reflected broad bipartisan support. His Gallup poll approval figures, which had stood at 51 percent on September 10, shot up to 90 percent by September 22, representing the highest presidential approval rating in U.S. history. The thirty-nine-point jump more than doubled the previous record—an eighteen-point boost his father, George H.W. Bush, received during Operation Desert Storm. A Gallup poll taken in early October 2002, one year after the start of Operation Enduring Freedom, showed a 67 percent approval rating for Bush. Although it was twenty-three points below his peak, it was clear that a large majority of Americans supported his leadership in the ongoing war against terrorism.

President Bush speaks to New York firefighters as he tours the site of the World Trade Center after the September 11 terrorist attacks.

Other nations almost universally expressed their sympathy for America and its loss. In London a special Changing of the Guard at Buckingham Palace was dedicated to the victims of the attacks, and a military band played the U.S. national anthem. British prime minister Tony Blair assured shaken Americans that his nation would support them:

> My father's generation went through the experience of the second world war, when Britain was under attack, during the days of the [German] Blitz. And there was one nation and one people that, above all, stood side by side with us at that time. And that nation was America, and those people were the American people. And I say to you, we stand side by side with you now, without hesitation.[26]

The nature of America's response became clear three days after the attacks when prominent politicians, including three former U.S. presidents, and government employees gathered for a memorial service at the National Cathedral in Washington. Religious leaders from all the major faiths gave invocations, and Bush followed with an address in which he offered yet another warning to those responsible for the attacks:

> Just three days removed from these events, Americans do not yet have the distance of history, but our responsibility to history is already clear: to answer these attacks and rid the world of evil. War has been waged against us by stealth and deceit and murder. This nation is peaceful, but fierce when stirred to anger. This conflict was begun on the timing and terms of others; it will end in a way and at an hour of our choosing.[27]

Afterward the president flew to New York City to meet with rescue workers and the families of the victims. There, he delivered an equally unambiguous message to al-Qaeda. Bush stood atop a platform amidst the rubble and began speaking to the thousands of workers. But when people began yelling that they could not hear him, the president shot back: "I hear you. The rest of the world hears you. And the people who knocked these buildings down will hear from all of us soon!"[28]

The Bush Doctrine

In the days and weeks following the attacks, patriotism swept the nation. Bush's tough talk about making no distinction between the terrorists and the governments that harbored them struck a chord in many Americans. A *Washington Post*–ABC News poll showed that 84 percent of the U.S. population supported military retaliation against countries that provided a haven for terrorists. The president's words did more than rally the public; they formed the basis of what came to be known as the Bush Doctrine—a policy that would rely on military preemption in dealing with rogue nations and state sponsors of terrorism. Never before had the United States made such a far-reaching declaration. The new doctrine clearly deviated from the concept of containment, under which the U.S. would respond if attacked but not strike first. The president's speech to a joint session of Congress on September 20 expanded on this theme when he announced:

We will pursue nations that provide aid or safe haven to terrorism. Every nation, in every region, now has a decision to make. Either you are with us, or you are with the terrorists. From this day forward, any nation that continues to harbor or support terrorism will be regarded by the United States as a hostile regime.[29]

The Bush Doctrine was interpreted differently by many people in Washington, even within the president's own administration. For example, Deputy Secretary of Defense Paul Wolfowitz took an aggressive stance, telling reporters that he was in favor of not simply punishing states that sponsored terrorism, but ending them. Secretary of State Colin Powell espoused a more moderate position, saying, "We're after ending terrorism. And if there are states and regimes, nations that support terrorism, we hope to persuade them that it is in their interest to stop doing that. But I think 'ending terrorism' is where I would like to leave it, and let Mr. Wolfowitz speak for himself."[30]

Bush gathered his national security team at Camp David to put the debate to rest. Wolfowitz lobbied for a broad campaign, one that included Iraq. Powell argued that an international coalition would only agree to join the fight if the enemy was al-Qaeda. With no firm proof of ties between al-Qaeda and Iraqi leader Saddam Hussein, a war council vote favored Powell's position. Phase one in the war against terrorism would indeed be against al-Qaeda and the main battlefield Afghanistan.

Building a Coalition

With the question settled of where the war on terrorism would begin, Powell's immediate task was to begin building an international coalition willing to join the United States in that fight. His job had been made considerably easier on September 12 when the North Atlantic Treaty Organization (NATO) for the first time in its fifty-two-year history invoked Article 5—the mutual defense provision—of the Washington Treaty. The provision stated that an armed attack against any member would be treated as an attack against all members. This meant that the United States could count on NATO member nations to support the war against terrorism militarily and/or logistically. The latter could be accomplished by a NATO member's agreeing to open its military bases to U.S. troops or to allow use of its airspace.

Powell's goal of involving the United Nations also was achieved in late September when the National Security Council passed Resolution 1373, which condemned the terrorist attacks on the United States.

Tony Blair: True Friend of America

British prime minister Tony Blair and President George W. Bush, two men from opposite ends of the political spectrum, forged a strong working relationship as well as a genuine friendship in the days and weeks following the terrorist attacks on the United States. Like Bush, Blair took a firm stand against terrorism. Shortly after learning of the horrific attacks on America, Blair told the British Parliament that terrorism "is the new evil in our world today. It is perpetrated by fanatics who are utterly indifferent to the sanctity of life and we, the democracies of this world, are going to have to come together and fight it together and eradicate this evil completely from our world." To show his country's immediate support after the attacks, Blair traveled to the United States and toured the destruction at the World Trade Center. He was a guest at Bush's historic September address to Congress and heard the president say that America had no greater friend than Great Britain. In the preparations for war, that message was borne out when Britain became America's strongest coalition partner. Blair's military

commanders worked with Pentagon officials in devising a military plan of attack, and the prime minister initially committed more than four thousand British troops to Afghanistan. The relationship that had formed between Blair and Bush ensured U.S. forces would not have to operate alone in the war against terrorism.

President Bush and Tony Blair forged a strong working relationship after the September 11 attacks.

The UN resolution also reaffirmed "the need to combat by all means, in accordance with the Charter of the United Nations, threats to international peace and security caused by terrorist acts."[31] The resolution was mainly symbolic, because under the Bush Doctrine the United States was prepared to act without UN approval. But among members of the international community, particularly Arab states suspicious of U.S. motives, UN involvement was critical, because it gave legitimacy to the upcoming war against terrorism.

Foreign leaders and ambassadors arrived in Washington throughout September to meet with Bush and Powell. Among the visitors was Tony Blair, who gave assurances that he would commit British troops in the impending war. Canada and Australia also pledged military support as the campaign unfolded. French president Jacques Chirac assured Bush of his country's support, as did China's foreign affairs minister, Tan Jiaxuan. Powell even enlisted America's former Cold War adversary, Russia, which agreed to provide vital information to military planners preparing for a war in Afghanistan.

Powell had been successful in enlisting many of America's traditional—and some nontraditional—allies in the looming conflict. Still, Powell viewed Pakistan as critical to the success of any operation the U.S. military undertook in Afghanistan. To launch air offenses into Afghanistan, American warplanes would require access to Pakistani airspace, and possibly its military bases. U.S. and coalition forces would also depend heavily on the Pakistani army to seal the border

The Special Forces A-Team

The Special Forces Operational Detachment Alpha—or A-Team—is the primary fighting unit of the U.S. Army's Special Forces and arguably the most elite group of combat-ready soldiers in the world. Each twelve-man A-Team is led by a captain; a warrant officer is second in command. Rounding out the team are two noncommissioned officers (NCOs) in each of the five Special Forces functional areas: communications, engineering, medical, operations and intelligence, and weapons. With two specialists in each set of operational skills, the unit is designed to function as two six-man teams, if necessary. Each soldier is also cross-trained in functional areas should he be required to replace a fellow trooper in an emergency. Moreover, the A-Teams are qualified to work with foreign militaries and train their soldiers. For all these reasons the members of this small but elite branch of the U.S. military became the first soldiers inserted into Afghanistan and were instrumental in eventually defeating the Taliban.

General Tommy Franks, in an interview on PBS's *Frontline*, praised the work of Special Forces members, calling them "young, capable, smart, dedicated. . . . [They were] introduced in the country of Afghanistan in a great many locations in very small numbers. It sounds a bit dramatic, but they were inserted in the dead of night, sort of alone, but unafraid. They took a great deal of capacity with them—a capacity to communicate, capacity to be able to identify and engage targets at a considerable distance from themselves, using air-to-ground forces, close air support. [It was] . . . a remarkable effort. I predict that people will still be writing about the exploits of some of these young people well off into the future."

to keep any Taliban and al-Qaeda fighters from escaping and also to prevent Pakistani sympathizers from crossing into Afghanistan to join the Taliban in the fight. Moreover, the CIA needed whatever intelligence on high-ranking al-Qaeda and Taliban operatives that Pakistani officials might have. But Pakistan's president, General Pervez Musharraf, was in a difficult position. His nation was home to hard-line religious leaders and militant Islamic groups that had links to the Taliban and who vehemently opposed helping the United States in any way. Powell promised Musharraf a steep increase in aid and hinted that U.S. sanctions against Pakistan resulting from the coup that had brought Musharraf to power would be dropped. The Pakistani president eventually agreed to many of the U.S. requests.

Although the U.S.-led coalition eventually numbered more than sixty nations, the proposed war on terrorism was not popular among countries in the Middle East. Many of the people in that region viewed the United States attack on Afghanistan as a Christian crusade against Islam. And many who remembered bin Laden's support for the mujahideen during the Russian occupation refused to believe that the al-Qaeda leader was guilty of planning the terrorist attacks on the United States. Bush attempted to win support in the Middle East when he spoke directly to Muslims in his September 20 speech to Congress:

We respect your faith. It's practiced freely by many millions of Americans, and by millions more in countries that America counts as friends. Its teachings are good and peaceful, and those who commit evil in the name of Allah blaspheme the name of Allah. The terrorists are traitors to their own faith, trying, in effect, to hijack Islam itself. The enemy of America is not our many Muslim friends; it is not our many Arab friends. Our enemy is a radical network of terrorists, and every government that supports them.[32]

A Battle Strategy Emerges

As Bush and Powell continued diplomatic efforts to expand the coalition, Secretary of Defense Donald Rumsfeld and the commander of U.S. Central Command (CENTCOM, the combat command responsible for military activity in Afghanistan), General Tommy Franks, worked on a comprehensive military strategy. Although the president initially wanted a large, conventional ground force in Afghanistan to punish the Taliban and al-Qaeda for the events of September 11, several arguments worked against such a strategy. The fiercely independent Afghan peoples would oppose a large invading army, as they had in the past. Another argument against a large ground force was that it could get bogged down in Afghanistan's mountainous terrain, where U.S. soldiers would be engaged in a war of attrition—that is, small battles and firefights that resulted in casualties but gained no territory. This prospect raised ugly memories of the Vietnam War, in which tens of thousands of American soldiers died in an unsuccessful attempt to prop up an unpopular regime. General Wesley Clark, former Supreme Allied Commander in Europe, dismissed the idea that Afghanistan would be another Vietnam since the objectives were far different: "Our soldiers can take care of themselves in any terrain. But, we also know that there is no inherent advantage in occupying Afghanistan. Our objective is to end international terrorism, not to conquer countries."[33]

In the end, Rumsfeld and Franks determined that the strategy in Afghanistan would be to use a relatively light but specialized ground force trained in counterterrorism tactics. Fighting the Taliban and al-Qaeda in the first phase of the war would, therefore, fall to the highly mobile U.S. Special Forces—Army Delta Force, Green Berets, Navy SEALs, and others. These commandos would locate and mark targets for U.S. warplanes and assist anti-Taliban forces inside the country. Military planners favored a strong partnership with the fifteen-thousand-strong Northern Alliance, who knew the land and the enemy well. The idea of fighting the Taliban and al-Qaeda and confining outsiders to a helping role appealed to Northern Alliance general Rashid Dostum, an ethnic Uzbek warlord, who said, "The terrain in Afghanistan devours people. The U.S. and NATO have to work with us. The U.S. should give us logistic support. We are ready to give them help in the region."[34]

Northern Alliance general Rashid Dostum agreed to help the United States fight al-Qaeda and the Taliban.

Although the war was expected to involve some pitched battles, much of the action would take place far from the public eye, and the CIA was also certain to play a vital role. In addition to freezing terrorists' bank accounts and partnering with other nations to gather intelligence on al-Qaeda, CIA operatives would be on the ground in Afghanistan collaborating with anti-Taliban forces, handing out money for their support, and bringing high-tech surveillance equipment to bear in the search for Osama bin Laden. According to reporter Bob Woodward, this use of covert forces was not a new concept:

> The CIA had covert relationships in Afghanistan authorized first in 1998 by Clinton and then reaffirmed later by him. The CIA was giving several million dollars a year in assistance to the Northern Alliance. The CIA also had contact with tribal leaders in southern Afghanistan. And the agency had secret paramilitary teams that had been going in and out of Afghanistan without detection for years to meet with opposition figures.[35]

Beating the Drums of War

The pieces were almost in place for an attack, but in his September 20 speech to Congress the president gave the Taliban leaders a chance to avert war:

> Deliver to United States authorities all the leaders of [al-Qaeda] who hide in your land. Close immediately and permanently every terrorist training camp in Afghanistan, and hand over every terrorist, and every person in their support structure, to appropriate author-

ities. Give the United States full access to terrorist training camps, so we can make sure they are no longer operating. These demands are not open to negotiation or discussion. The Taliban must act, and act immediately. They will hand over the terrorists, or they will share in their fate.[36]

Yet as the president spoke that night, U.S. military forces were already moving toward Afghanistan. The aircraft carrier USS *Theodore Roosevelt* and its associated battle group departed from its Norfolk, Virginia, base and headed east toward the Mediterranean Sea. The USS *Kitty Hawk* left Japan for the Persian Gulf, joining two more aircraft carriers already in the region—the USS *Enterprise* and USS *Carl Vinson*. Meanwhile several B-52 and B-1 bombers took off from various air force bases around the United States and flew to air bases in the region, joining combat aircraft stationed in Saudi Arabia, Kuwait, and Bahrain. The Twenty-sixth Marine Expeditionary Unit, in Egypt participating in a multinational military exercise, was also quickly deployed to the Afghan theater, and would later join up with the Fifteenth Marine Expeditionary Unit en route to the Arabian Sea from Australia. Three guided-missile destroyers were on the way, and the Pentagon readied the army's Eighteenth Airborne Corps, which included the Eighty-second Airborne Division. Army Rangers, Green Berets, and Navy SEALs were to join other elite fighting forces already in position.

In response to this massive military buildup, the Taliban hastily constructed bunkers and installed antiaircraft batteries. U.S.-made Stinger missiles, left over from the war against the Soviets, were readied for use. The Taliban called for volunteers to defend Afghan villages and valleys, and thousands of Pakistanis, determined to aid their Muslim brethren, crossed the border. Abdul Ali, a student from the Pakistani city of Peshawar, typified the prevailing attitude among the radical Muslims living in the region when he warned: "If America kills Osama, every Muslim is Osama. If America attacks Afghanistan, we will attack America."[37]

With American forces moving ever nearer, the Taliban ambassador to Pakistan, Mullah Abdul Salam Zaeef, finally answered Bush's September 20 demand, saying, "Osama is in Afghanistan, but he is at an unknown place for his safety and security. Only security people know about his whereabouts. Osama bin Laden is under our control."[38] American policy makers took Zaeef's statement to mean that the Taliban were not going to deliver bin Laden, so the buildup to war continued.

Elite Forces Enter Afghanistan

The large force heading for Afghanistan would join other forces already in the region. Just days after the attacks of September 11, Special Forces and CIA operatives had secretly entered Afghanistan. By late September teams consisting of SEALs, Green Berets, Delta Force, and CIA-trained paramilitary personnel were at work, under the command of the Joint Special Operations Command and the CIA. British Special Air Service (SAS) commandos were also on the ground in Afghanistan. The initial mission of the U.S. and British special ops teams was primarily surveillance—looking for and identifying targets for potential air strikes.

At the same time, small teams of CIA operatives were making contacts with Afghan

In September 2001, Mullah Abdul Salam Zaeef revealed that Osama bin Laden was hiding in Afghanistan.

citizens and gathering intelligence on bin Laden and Mullah Omar. But no sign of the al-Qaeda leader had been detected since shortly after the attacks of September 11. Teams of three to five soldiers aboard Black Hawk helicopters scoured the mountainous regions looking for him as well, but his location remained a mystery. Pakistan's Inter-Services Intelligence (ISI) reported that to elude capture bin Laden was moving daily to new locations between the Afghan cities of Kandahār and Jalālābād. "Only we know where Osama is," said Zaeef. "He is in a safe location where he will not be found, not by George Bush, not the special forces, not by anyone."[39] Maulana Sami ul-Haq, chancellor of the Dar-ul-Uloom Haqquania Muslim school in Peshawar and a close friend of bin Laden, added, "The Americans are never going to find or defeat Osama. If he could outwit the Soviets, he can do the same to the Americans. Tell the [U.S.] special forces they are wasting their time."[40]

By October 3 preparations for the attack were nearly complete. Only last-minute agreements with Afghanistan's neighbors for use of their military installations remained to be nailed down. The final arrangement came two days later when Uzbekistan gave the Pentagon approval to use several military bases, including a former Soviet air base in Karshi, one hundred miles north of the Afghan border. In the early stages of the war, this base would serve as headquarters for the Joint Special Operations Task Force—the primary U.S. fighting force in Afghanistan. In one last prelude to war, the United States ordered the Northern Alliance to clear its airspace for U.S. warplanes and missiles.

The Taliban made one effort to prevent the impending attack, offering to try bin Laden in an Afghan court under Islamic law for the terrorist attacks against the United States. White House spokesman Scott McClellan responded tersely, "The president's demands [for bin Laden's handover] are clear and nonnegotiable."[41] With any chance to avoid war now past, U.S. military personnel throughout the region were put on high alert. Northern Alliance troops were told to hold their positions. All that was needed was the order from the commander in chief to begin launching air strikes. The world collectively watched and waited.

✯ Chapter 4 ✯

Operation Enduring Freedom Begins

The stakes in the Afghan war were great, because if the U.S.-led campaign were to fail, al-Qaeda would likely regroup and begin planning other attacks against the United States, and the Taliban regime would continue their brutal reign over the Afghan people. But the battle would not be easy. The enemy was unknown, and the land was inhospitable. Moreover the bitter-cold Afghan winter—where temperatures fell to thirty degrees below zero—was just a few months away.

Three Objectives

The U.S. military had three main objectives in the war in Afghanistan. First was the elimination of Taliban air defenses so that American warplanes could fly unimpeded. This would be accomplished with a highly targeted but open-ended air campaign. A second objective was to provide effective air and ground support for the anti-Taliban forces collaborating with U.S. Special Forces to capture Taliban-held cities once the ground campaign started. If those two

objectives were met, U.S. and British Special Forces, along with anti-Taliban forces, could focus on the third and most important objective: hunting for bin Laden and his operatives.

The day of reckoning for Afghanistan arrived on October 7, just twenty-six days after Osama bin Laden and al-Qaeda had launched their attack on America. At 12:41 P.M. White House press secretary Ari Fleischer made this brief announcement from his media room podium: "Ladies and gentlemen, we are beginning another front in our war against terrorism, so freedom can prevail over fear."[42] Operation Enduring Freedom had begun.

Even before Fleischer spoke, American warplanes were heading toward the darkened skies over Afghanistan, directed by air commanders at the Combined Air Operations Center in Riyadh, Saudia Arabia. Fifty Tomahawk cruise missiles were launched from U.S. Navy ships and from British submarines. Twenty-five carrier-based warplanes—Navy F/A-18 and F-14 fighters—streaked in from the Arabian Sea. Another thirteen land-based bombers that had taken off from the island of Diego Garcia in the Indian Ocean were also on the way. In addition, a pair of B-2 Spirit stealth bombers were flying nonstop from Whiteman Air Force Base in Missouri, more than seven thousand miles away.

Shortly after the air campaign began, Bush appeared on national television to announce the start of the war against terror:

> On my orders, the United States military has begun strikes against al-Qaeda terrorist training camps and military

"Smarter" Bombs

The laser-guided bomb (LGB) used in Operation Desert Storm in 1991 was the first generation of so-called smart bombs. Either a special operator on the ground or the pilot of the aircraft "painted" the target with a laser. The LGB was launched from the aircraft, locked onto the laser, and struck its target. Although LGBs were quite accurate and reduced the number of civilian casualties from past wars that utilized conventional gravity, or "dumb," bombs, pilots ran into a visibility problem when clouds or sandstorms over Iraq obstructed the target. After Desert Storm the military began developing the next generation of smart bombs, which added satellite technology to the existing laser-guidance system. The result was a bomb equipped with a Global Positioning System (GPS). These bombs were called Joint Direct Attack Munitions (JDAMs). Because the GPS uses radio waves, which cloud cover does not affect, JDAMs worked in all weather conditions. This was critical during the winter in Afghanistan, when dense clouds often hid the terrain from a pilot's view. Even under heavy cloud cover, once the bomb was dropped, its Inertial Navigation System (INS) communicated with the GPS to pinpoint its target. About 60 percent of all bombs dropped in Operation Enduring Freedom were precision-guided bombs, and many used the sophisticated satellite guidance for maximum accuracy.

But smart bombs did not always work the way they were designed to work. Whether due to human or computer error, bombs veered off course from time to time, and because the Taliban often took up positions close to civilian areas, the consequences were sometimes deadly. Although the Taliban almost certainly exaggerated civilian casualty figures, some analysts believe between one thousand and thirteen hundred innocent Afghans died in the bombing campaign.

U.S. aircraft personnel load a smart bomb onto the wing of a fighter jet.

installations of the Taliban regime in Afghanistan. These carefully targeted actions are designed to disrupt the use of Afghanistan as a terrorist base of operations, and to attack the military capability of the Taliban regime. We are joined in this operation by our staunch friend, Great Britain. . . . Initially, the terrorists may burrow deeper into caves and other entrenched hiding places. Our military action is also designed to clear the way for sustained, comprehensive and relentless operations to drive them out and bring them to justice. . . . We will not waver; we will not tire; we will not falter; and we will not fail.[43]

Gaining an Air Advantage

Forty U.S. warplanes targeted thirty-one sites the first night, quite a small operation in comparison with other modern U.S. air campaigns. For example, as part of Operation Desert Storm, in which coalition forces ejected Iraqi troops from Kuwait in 1991, more than 650 aircraft flew 1,322 sorties the first night. In Afghanistan, the lack of Taliban military infrastructure meant that massive bombing was not warranted. Nevertheless, exploding bombs shook areas across Afghanistan all through the night. The first wave of bombs ripped through Taliban air defense systems, causing massive explosions and clearing the way for additional bombing missions in the days and weeks to come. The lightning offensive rocked Kandahār, where U.S. precision-

guided bombs shredded a Taliban command system and radar station at the airport. Mullah Omar's home and an al-Qaeda housing complex in Kandahār were also targeted. Strategic sites around Kabul were struck, including the airport, Taliban political and military bases, and several training bases. Near the northern city of Mazar-e Sharif, Taliban tanks and armored vehicles were destroyed. Command-and-control bunkers around Kabul were hit with five thousand-pound Guided Bomb Unit-28s (GBU-28s), called "bunker busters." The bombs pierced the concrete and steel structures, traveling more than fifty feet underground before detonating. The huge explosions shattered the bunkers and instantly killed their occupants.

Meanwhile, Tomahawk cruise missiles launched from American ships and British submarines streaked low across the horizon and found their targets: bin Laden's suspected training camps. The American aerial bombardment lasted for more than six hours the first night, during which the Taliban managed only sporadic antiaircraft gunfire. They never attempted to send up their two dozen or so Soviet-era MiG-21 and SU-22 fighter aircraft, which were no match for the American planes. Despite the overwhelming U.S. dominance in the air, Defense Secretary Rumsfeld remained cautious in his assessment of the ability of aerial bombardment to defeat the enemy:

It is very unlikely that the air strikes will rock the Taliban back on their heels. We have to have a clear understanding of

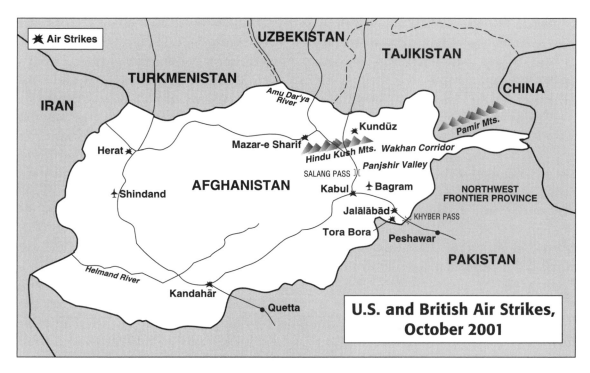

U.S. and British Air Strikes, October 2001

what is possible in a country like that. The Soviet Union pounded it year after year after year. Much of the country is rubble. They [the Taliban] do not have high-value targets or assets that are the kinds of things that would lend themselves to substantial damage from the air. These raids are just one small part of the entire effort. The cruise missiles and bombers are not going to solve this problem. We know that. It is not simple. It is not neat. There is no silver bullet.[44]

Air Raids Intensify

Rumsfeld's comments seemed borne out when, shortly after the United States initiated air strikes in Afghanistan, Osama bin Laden broke his long silence. The Arab satellite news channel Al-Jazeera broadcast videotape showing Osama bin Laden with his top lieutenant, Ayman al-Zawahiri, and spokesman Sulaiman Abu-Ghaith. The broadcast was quickly picked up and aired by television stations in the United States. In a message that was clearly designed to strike fear in Americans, bin Laden threatened that "neither America nor the people who live in it will dream of security before we live it in Palestine, and not before all the infidel armies leave the land of Muhammad [Saudi Arabia]."[45] Al-Zawahiri added:

People of America, your government is leading you into a losing battle. Remember that your government was defeated in Vietnam, fled in panic from Lebanon, rushed out of Somalia and was slapped across the face in [Yemen]. Your government today is leading you into a losing war, where you will lose your sons and your money.[46]

At home, the FBI, fearful that these communiqués contained coded messages ordering more attacks by al-Qaeda operatives in the United States, called on more than eighteen thousand law enforcement organizations and twenty-seven thousand corporate security managers to be on the highest level of alert against possible terrorist attacks.

Meanwhile, all aircraft used on the first night of the bombing campaign returned safely to their respective bases and carriers. Intelligence reports showed they had knocked out the Taliban's long-range surface-to-air missile sites and struck a combination of Taliban and al-Qaeda troops near Mazar-e Sharif. The next night, air strikes resumed, though on a smaller scale. Only ten carrier-based fighter planes and five bombers were used, and American and British navy vessels launched fewer cruise missiles. Once again the bombs and missiles were aimed at specific targets, including Taliban air defenses and cave hideouts. Bin Laden's training camp near Farmada, south of Jalālābād, was hit, as were Taliban and al-Qaeda troop concentrations in Kabul, Kandahār, Kunduz, and Mazar-e Sharif. By the third day, 85 percent of the targets on the Pentagon's initial list had been destroyed, and American aircraft were flying bombing missions around the clock.

Psyching Out the Taliban

Psychological Operations, or PsyOps for short, have historically been used in times of war to gain a mental advantage against the enemy. In Operation Enduring Freedom, the army's Fourth Psychological Operations Group utilized two main techniques to do just that against the Taliban: dropping propaganda leaflets and broadcasting pro-American information over the radio. One of the first propaganda leaflets used to cast doubt in the minds of Taliban troops was dropped near their frontline positions. The leaflets warned them not to fight and gave instructions on how to surrender peacefully. Illustrating what would happen otherwise was an image of a Taliban soldier taking an offensive posture and coming under attack by a U.S. warplane. Another leaflet instructed the Taliban to tune their radios to receive broadcasts from "Commando Solo," a U.S. Air Force Special Operations EC-130 flying high above. One of the messages announced, "Attention, Taliban. You are condemned. Did you know? The instant the terrorists you support took over our planes, you sentenced yourselves to death."

The army's PsyOps group did not target the enemy alone, however. One of the keystones to success in Operation Enduring Freedom was convincing non-Taliban Afghans that they were not the enemy in this conflict and that the coalition was there to liberate them. To wage this "battle," PsyOps once again used radio broadcasts and leaflets. One of the leaflets showed an American soldier shaking hands with a local Afghan. Printed on the leaflet were the words, "The Partnership of Nations Is Here to Help."

A Battle for Afghan Hearts and Minds

As fierce as the aerial bombardment was, areas with heavy populations had been intentionally left off U.S. target lists so as to avoid civilian casualties. Still, on the first night of air strikes, there were some deadly mishaps. For example, a smart bomb veered off course and struck a civilian area, reportedly killing up to twenty Afghan civilians. Days later a UN warehouse was accidentally struck by a bomb, killing four volunteers. The Taliban took advantage of such accidents using them to back their claims that the U.S.-led air strikes were a terrorist attack.

The Taliban's intent was to spark anger in the Arab and Muslim world, just as the Soviet invasion of Afghanistan had done in 1979, and to some extent the strategy worked. Pakistanis supportive of the Taliban rose up in Islamabad and violently protested the U.S. air strikes. Many Arabs in the Middle East also took to the streets in anger. Powell and others at the U.S. State Department busily worked the diplomatic phone lines with Arab and Muslim government officials to keep the protests from damaging the fragile coalition.

Of greater concern for American forces operating in Afghanistan, however, was the temperament of ordinary Afghans, whose country was under attack. Pentagon officials believed that the success of a war in Afghanistan depended in large measure on winning the hearts and minds of the people. The coalition tried to do that by dropping food packages to thousands of starving Afghan refugees. The humanitarian missions also included dropping medicines and blankets. Ike Skelton, a congressman from Missouri, was impressed with the U.S. goal of feeding hungry Afghans while bombing the Taliban. "It's the first time I've ever heard of trying to feed the people while you're trying to destroy their government," he said. "I don't think it's ever been done before, but I think it's an excellent strategy." [47]

The humanitarian aid mission was just one phase of the overall plan to win over the Afghan people. Early in the campaign, the army's Fourth Psychological Operations (PsyOps) Group dropped millions of leaflets showing a portrait of a U.S. soldier and an Afghan civilian shaking hands, an image designed to convey the friendly intentions of Americans toward civilians. PsyOps also dropped leaflets announcing a reward of up to $25 million for information leading to the capture of bin Laden or his lieutenant, al-Zawahiri. Meanwhile, the 193rd Special Operations Wing flew an EC-130 aircraft broadcasting pro-American radio transmissions to Afghans. The radio message read in part:

> We are here to take measures against terrorists who have rooted themselves in your country. It is not you, the honorable people of Afghanistan, who are targeted, but those who oppress you, seek to bend you to their will, and make you their slaves. [48]

In the second week of U.S. air strikes, pilots struck the Taliban's military headquarters near the Jalālābād airport and a bin Laden training camp in the mountains of Tora Bora. And for the first time the low-flying AC-130 "gun ships" flew inside Afghanistan and punished Taliban troops, convoys, and other mobile targets around Kandahār with cannon and heavy machine-gun fire. Attacking their southern stronghold dealt the Taliban a severe blow and reinforced the message to Mullah Omar that he was being targeted personally. On October 15 at a press conference in Washington, Bush commented on the apparent success of the air campaign: "[We're] disrupting their networks, we're destroying their camps, we've got them on the run and we're going to keep them on the run."[49]

Special Forces Team Enters Afghanistan

The overall goal of the air campaign was to weaken the Taliban so that their opponents, the Northern Alliance, could make headway in retaking territory and thus drive the Taliban from power. At the start of Operation Enduring Freedom, however, prospects for achieving this were not good. Taliban militias controlled about 90 percent of Afghan land, leaving the Northern Alliance pinned inside northeastern territories mainly along the borders of Tajikistan and Uzbekistan. The Afghan resistance force was a splintered army, with roughly fifteen thousand soldiers divided among five factions and possibly as many as twenty-five subfactions. The men had limited numbers of weapons and insufficient food and winter clothing. The North-

ern Alliance had also recently lost its renowned leader Ahmed Shah Massoud, legendary for repelling the Soviets several times at Panjshir Valley in the 1980s. He had been assassinated by al-Qaeda two days before the September 11 attacks.

Bin Laden had calculated that the United States—if and when it retaliated— would not be able to depend on a disorganized Northern Alliance force to fight the Taliban and al-Qaeda. In the first days of the war, bin Laden's strategy appeared to be working, at least according to reporter Steve Harrigan, covering the war in Afghanistan:

A look at the front line positions of the Northern Alliance reveals an army very ill-prepared to begin any offensive. No sense of communications between different posts. No electricity at the posts. No transportation between the posts, and a real mix of weapons—Soviet, Russian, Chinese, American, with few spare parts to be had. If this army is going to work with the U.S., it's going to need a lot of help very quickly.[50]

Not only were the opposition groups at a logistical disadvantage, they were not necessarily prepared to work together. The situation required a team of highly trained U.S. commandos to help the Afghan opposition groups, consisting of ethnic Uzbeks and Tajiks, work together and turn them into a force capable of defeating the Taliban and tracking down bin Laden. The first

Northern Alliance general Mohammed Fahim inspects his troops. U.S. Special Forces worked with Fahim to secure control of Bagram Air Base.

team chosen for the task was Army Special Forces A-Team 555, the Green Berets. Military scholar Robin Moore explains the diverse talents of this force:

> There is no fighting unit in the world like the U.S. Army Special Forces A-Team. If enemy attrition is your goal, i.e., killing the bad guys, then Special Forces are the men for the job. The U.S. Army Special Forces are able to field the most completely cross-trained fighting men and diplomats of any military unit in the history of warfare.[51]

On October 19, Team 555 secretly flew into Afghanistan aboard two army UH-47 helicopters and was dropped deep in northern Afghanistan. Like other Special Forces to follow, the team included twelve commandos, two CIA operatives, and an air force Special Operations combat controller, who would be responsible for directing U.S. aircraft to their targets. Wearing night-vision goggles and carrying three hundred pounds of equipment among them, the men trekked over miles of rugged and unfamiliar terrain to meet up with Northern Alliance general Mohammed Fahim. The commandos immediately set out south in search of targets for air strikes in the Taliban front line around Bagram Air Base, the old Russian-built airstrip near Kabul. Fahim's forces controlled the northern half of the air base, and the Taliban held the southern half. Securing the entire air base would be a key prerequisite to seizing Kabul.

The Infiltration Continues

Shortly after the first team of special operatives arrived inside Afghanistan, another group of commandos, Team 595, hit the ground fifty miles south of Mazar-e Sharif, a Taliban stronghold in the north. According to Moore, there was plenty of responsibility riding on their shoulders:

> The Special Forces team was to infiltrate and conduct the main attack in the effort to capture Mazar-e Sharif. A victory would seize a key airbase, open a road to Uzbekistan, shake the very spine of the Taliban and al-Qaida, and hopefully have a cascading effect on the enemy in the north, causing a roll-up in subsequent battles.[52]

Team 595 joined General Rashid Dostum's forces and traveled toward the Taliban front lines around Mazar-e Sharif. When they reached their destination, the special ops immediately called for close air support from warplanes circling above the region. The first bomb to land obliterated a Taliban bunker, bringing loud cheers from the Northern Alliance troops. Over the next few days the Green Berets settled into a working relationship with their Alliance partners. The Americans acquired horses from local Afghans and rode alongside Dostum and his men, who often resorted to cavalry-style charges against the Taliban. As Team 595 identified targets for U.S. warplanes, Dostum and his men would wait for the bomb to detonate and then charge furiously toward their Taliban opponents with guns blazing.

Similar fighting continued for the next ten days, though not every battle was a success. For example, in one major Alliance offensive Dostum's men stormed a Taliban-held hill, only to be ambushed by Taliban in tanks and personnel carriers hidden on the far slope. In response, the Special Forces team split into four groups and traveled behind enemy lines to positions around and beside the mountain and then called in heavy air strikes directly on top of Taliban tanks and personnel carriers. The strategy used in this early battle became an important model for defeating enemy forces in the mountains of Afghanistan. By the end of October, Team 595 had killed more than 125 Taliban soldiers and captured nearly as many, while losing only 8 men. More important, however, the U.S. commandos and their Afghan partners were advancing on Mazar-e Sharif at a clip of ten to thirty kilometers a day.

An Afghanistan Quagmire?

By the time the air campaign entered its fourth week, most of the Taliban air defense had been decimated. American aircraft, working with the two Special Forces A-Teams on the ground, began targeting Taliban armored columns and troop reinforcements well behind the front lines. The strategy at this point was to cut off supplies to frontline troops. However, although the close coordination between Special Forces on the ground and air force and navy pilots in the air was having some effect in terms of punishing and confusing the Taliban, success measured by the surrender of large numbers of the enemy was not forthcoming. For example, the Northern Alliance force at

Bagram Air Base had engaged the Taliban with fierce gunfire for nearly two weeks, and yet the enemy appeared to be holding strong.

The military's apparent struggles drew increasing media attention. Newspaper columnists also began questioning whether Americans were prepared for a longer battle than anticipated. One columnist in the *New York Times*, R.W. Apple Jr., raised the specter of large numbers of American troops being drawn into a losing battle, as had happened decades earlier in Vietnam:

> Is the United States facing another stalemate on the other side of the world? Premature the questions may be, three weeks after the fighting began. Unreasonable they are not, given the scars scoured into the national psyche by defeat in Southeast Asia. For all the differences between the two conflicts, and there are many, echoes of Vietnam are unavoidable. Today, for example, Defense Secretary Donald H. Rumsfeld disclosed for the first time that American military forces are operating in northern Afghanistan, providing liaison to "a limited number of the various opposition elements." Their role sounds suspiciously like that of the advisers sent to Vietnam in the early 1960's. . . . The U.S. government of the day vigorously denied that they [the advisers] were a prelude to American combat troops.[53]

Few people in the Bush administration considered Afghanistan another Vietnam, but there was some concern that the Northern Alliance was not moving fast enough, and that perhaps another plan that included more U.S. ground troops should be considered. National security adviser Condoleezza Rice, one member of the administration concerned about the lack of progress made against the Taliban, met privately with the president on October 25. She sought Bush's assurance that he still had confidence in the plan. Although the Taliban had showed resiliency thus far, the president was convinced they would eventually collapse under the relentless American airpower. To put the matter to rest, the next morning, during the National Security Council meeting, Bush asked the council members if they were still in favor of carrying out the original plan. Vice President Richard Cheney, Secretary of State Powell, CIA director Tenet, Rice, and others all signaled their support. Confident his team was making the right decision, the president then told everyone in attendance:

> We need to be patient. We've got a good plan. Look, we're entering a difficult phase. The press will seek to find divisions among us. They will try and force on us a strategy that is not consistent with victory. We've been at this only 19 days. Be steady. Don't let the press panic us. Resist the second-guessing. . . . We've got to be cool and steady. It's all going to work.[54]

After three weeks of war, the United States ruled the skies and was increasing the

U.S. General Tommy Franks

General Tommy R. Franks was born in Wynnewood, Oklahoma, on June 17, 1945. His family later moved to Midland, Texas, where he attended high school. Franks's military career began in 1965 when he dropped out of the University of Texas and joined the army, and with war raging in Vietnam it was not long before he saw action. In 1967 Franks served the first of his three tours of duty as an artillery lieutenant. After earning three Purple Hearts for combat wounds in Vietnam, Franks rose rapidly through the military ranks, commanding an armored engineer company in West Germany and then serving as assistant division commander of the First Cavalry Division during Operation Desert Storm. A decade later he was named commander of the U.S. Central Command and was responsible for military operations against the Taliban and Osama bin Laden's terrorist network inside Afghanistan.

Early in the Afghanistan campaign, Franks found himself compared to one of his predecessors, General Norman Schwarzkopf. However, unlike Schwarzkopf, who was comfortable as a public personality, Franks preferred a lower profile. When reporters complained to Franks about his infrequent appearances in front of the media, Franks responded to them with humor: "Tommy Franks is no Norman Schwarzkopf." Criticism of Franks was not limited to reporters, however. Many military analysts expected Franks, as a former infantryman, to utilize a heavy ground force in Afghanistan. He instead settled on using a limited but very specialized ground force to accompany a targeted air campaign. When the Taliban stood strong in the face of overwhelming U.S. airpower early on in the campaign, the level of

criticism rose. But the detractors quickly saw the wisdom in Franks's strategy when the Taliban began to crumble under the relentless attack. While Franks was no Norman Schwarzkopf when it came to addressing the media, he certainly proved to be the former commander's equal in conducting effective military operations.

General Tommy Franks talks with reporters about the war in Afghanistan.

pressure on the Taliban with an even heavier concentration of smart and conventional bombs. The attacks flushed out Taliban armored personnel carriers and tanks as they attempted to reinforce battered troups, which made them easier targets. Little by little, U.S. warplanes were taking out Taliban

defenses, and the war was beginning to shift in the coalition's favor. But the secrecy that defined this war kept any progress from the public eye, and to Americans it did indeed appear that the U.S. military was becoming bogged down in Afghanistan. That perception, however, would soon change.

Chapter 5

The Sudden Taliban Collapse

By early November the first phase of the war was mostly complete. Taliban air defense installations had been greatly degraded, though not entirely eliminated. American warplanes continued targeting air defenses wherever they could be found, but, by and large, air sorties against Taliban troop concentrations became the order of the day. Despite the progress that had been made, much remained to be done. Enemy troop concentrations around Kabul and Mazar-e Sharif appeared strong, and relentless bombing would be required to force their imminent and complete collapse.

The Problem of Ramadan

One of the problems facing the U.S.-led military effort at the one-month mark of the campaign was that the Muslim holy month of Ramadan was two weeks away and leaders of nations with large Muslim populations were calling for a pause in the action. Continuing the campaign threatened to put a strain on the coalition, particularly because most Pakistanis, including President Musharraf, were against doing so. But pausing or dramatically decreasing military action would risk giving up precious gains. Northern Alliance forces stood poised to begin the final push toward Mazar-e Sharif and Kabul. The Pentagon resolved the Ramadan issue when a statement was broadcast in fifty-three languages over the official radio service, Voice of America: "The coalition has no choice but to go to the source of the terrorism in Afghanistan and to root out terrorist groups elsewhere. As President George W. Bush put it, 'the enemy won't rest during Ramadan, and neither will we.'"[55]

Additional Special Forces units were entering the fray. By early November two more A-Teams were operating inside Afghanistan. Team 585 was paired with a Northern Alliance force and moving toward Kunduz, the Taliban's main stronghold in the north. Team 534 joined Northern Alliance commander Ustad Mohammed Atta east of

Mazar-e Sharif, with the intention of coordinating Northern Alliance troop movement in the final assault on that city.

Meanwhile, Team 595 had built a solid rapport with Dostum and his soldiers, and they were prepared to start their advance toward Mazar-e Sharif. Standing in their way, however, were heavy Taliban and al-Qaeda defenses—thousands of troops, along with tanks, personnel carriers, and rocket-propelled grenades. But with heavy air support from B-52 bombers, Dostum's men continued their advance. With winter setting in, however, the battle grew more dif-

Unmanned Aerial Vehicle

Before the first bomb was dropped in Operation Enduring Freedom, Predator Unmanned Aerial Vehicles (UAVs) were circling high above Afghanistan, feeding target data to military commanders. Once the war started, UAVs became even more important. In the rugged mountains of Afghanistan, where travel by foot was extremely difficult, coalition ground troops relied heavily on Predators for surveillance and reconnaissance. Equipped with radar, video cameras, and infrared detectors, more than ten Predators flew continuously at altitudes between fifteen thousand and twenty-five thousand feet above the battlefield for more than thirty hours at a time. Both the air force and CIA used Predators to track enemy movement and transmit photos in real time to U.S. commanders on the front lines. Often Predators were used in combat situations as well. In November 2001, for example, a Predator pinpointed a house sheltering several senior al-Qaeda officials, including the terrorist network's military commander, Muhammad Atef. The UAV transmitted live pictures of the scene to CIA and military officials, who then called in a navy F/A-18 fighter-bomber for air strikes. As terrorists fled the scene, the Predator fired its Hellfire missiles. Atef and others were killed in the raid.

Technicians prepare a Predator UAV for a surveillance mission above Afghanistan.

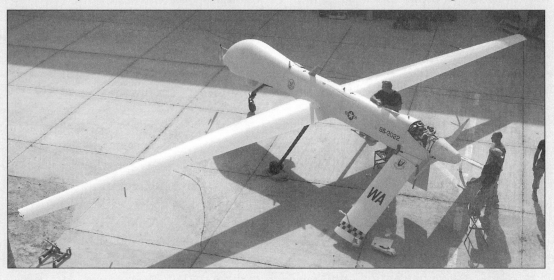

ficult. Low visibility made it harder to target Taliban troops positioned far in the distance. To solve the problem, Team 595 called on a Predator Unmanned Aerial Vehicle (UAV). Equipped with high-tech sensors, including an infrared camera and radar, the Predator beamed images of the battlefield to an operator at the air command center in Saudi Arabia. The operator in turn sent coordinates of Taliban troop positions to pilots nearby, who then fired missiles. With such close air support the men pushed forward.

Now, as pockets of Taliban resistance began to collapse, a new problem arose: what to do with captured enemy soldiers. Knowing defeat was at hand, many Afghan Taliban fighters switched sides and took up arms with the Northern Alliance. But a great many others who were still considered hostile—mainly soldiers from the largely Muslim Russian province of Chechnya and Pakistan—had to be dealt with, and growing numbers of prisoners of war threatened to slow the advance. To solve the problem, Dostum's men had little choice but to conduct cursory weapons searches before transporting the captives to a nearby prison called Qala-i-Jangi.

The First to Fall

To speed the Northern Alliance advance on Mazar-e Sharif, U.S. commanders now elected to drop Vietnam-era BLU-82B "daisy cutter" bombs on Taliban frontline positions. In Vietnam the massive bombs had often been used to clear huge swaths in the dense jungle terrain for helicopter landing

To help the Northern Alliance advance on Mazar-e Sharif, U.S. commanders dropped massive daisy cutter bombs on Taliban positions.

zones and to deprive enemy fighters of hiding places. But in Afghanistan these weapons were used solely for the purpose of inflicting heavy casualties on Taliban troops, as General Peter Pace explains:

> They are 15,000-pound bombs that literally fit on a pallet on a C-130. They're pushed out of the back of the C-130 and float down by parachute. They have a probe that sticks out, so when the probe hits the ground, they explode about three feet above the ground. And as you would expect, they make a heck of a bang when they go off, and the intent is to kill people.[56]

The massive damage inflicted by the daisy cutter bombs left many Taliban troops unable—and unwilling—to fight, and on

November 6, Dostum's forces seized Taliban-controlled land in the Zari district just south of Mazar-e Sharif. This turned out to be a key acquisition of enemy territory in that it started a chain reaction that caused the Taliban to lose their grip on Mazar-e Sharif. As Northern Alliance troops moved into positions on mountain ridges overlooking the city, the Taliban began fleeing in large convoys. The special operators then called in smart bombs. Alliance troops watching from high above "were simply ecstatic," says Green Beret Max Bowers. "We saturated the battlefield with small close-air-support cells and we hit the Taliban if they were engaging us, if they were trying to maneuver in a favorable position. We engaged them while they were moving and if they tried to retreat. They simply could not move."[57]

Any Taliban soldiers who made it out of Mazar-e Sharif traveled east to Kunduz or made their way south toward Kabul. By November 9, Mazar-e Sharif had fallen to Alliance forces, and Dostum received a hero's welcome from citizens of the city. But one unresolved problem threatened to plunge the city back into chaos: Eight hundred mostly Pakistani Taliban were holed up inside a Muslim school outside the city and were refusing to surrender. To deal with the problem, Special Forces surrounded the building and held the occupants under siege. Then they called for pinpoint air strikes that ripped through the top of the building, killing more than half inside. The situation was soon back under coalition control. Meanwhile, by November 12, the North-ern Alliance had captured Herat without a fight. The Taliban were clearly in a free-fall. In a month of fighting that had produced few positive outcomes, news of the sudden collapse of the two Taliban-held cities was met with broad approval in the United States. The word *quagmire* would no longer be used to describe the American involvement in Afghanistan.

The Rout Is On

Dostum and his men reveled in their victory at Mazar-e Sharif, but the Alliance leader soon turned his attention to Kabul. Other Alliance commanders who had fought in the north set their sights on the capital as well. The rapid advance on Kabul alarmed Pakistan president Musharraf, who feared what ethnic Tajik and Uzbek elements within the Northern Alliance might do if and when the Taliban were defeated there. Musharraf cautioned, "Why I [am] recommending Kabul not be occupied by [the] Northern Alliance basically is because of the past experience that we've had when the various ethnic groups were in hold of Kabul after the Soviets left. There was total atrocity and killing and mayhem within the city. If the Northern Alliance enters Kabul, we'll see the same kind of atrocities being perpetuated."[58] Recognizing the strain that would be put on America's relations with a key coalition partner if Alliance forces were to occupy Kabul, President Bush attempted to ease Musharraf's concern by encouraging Alliance commanders to keep heading south and not enter the city itself.

Keeping the Northern Alliance armies out of Kabul would be difficult because of the clear boost to morale that capturing the city would impart. Furthermore, every Northern Alliance commander wanted his troops to have the honor of entering Kabul first. Abdul Rab Rusul Sayyaf, an authority in the Alliance Leadership Council, explains why Kabul meant so much:

> If we collect 20 Mazar-e Sharifs, it is not the same as breaking this [Kabul] line. If it falls, then the Taliban will fall down very quickly. Kabul is like the head of the enemy, and when you hit him in the head, his hands and feet cannot move.[59]

Indeed, the wishes of Bush and Musharraf were not heeded in the end. The Green Berets who had been at Bagram airfield since October 19 pressed General Fahim to be the first to charge into the capital. With Mazar-e Sharif and Herat no longer requiring American airpower, the team had an array of U.S. aircraft at their disposal to support their assault. On November 10 the Green Beret team called in twenty-five air strikes on Taliban troops, tanks, and command-and-control bunkers. The strikes killed more than twenty-two hundred enemy soldiers and provided an opening for Alliance soldiers. The next morning Fahim's force carried out a tested battlefield maneuver to storm Kabul, as described by Robin Moore:

> A large part of [Fahim's] force broke to the east and went straight toward the back side of Kabul. It was a classic single envelopment. The Taliban panicked. General Fahim's spies in Kabul relayed that they were fleeing with everything they owned. By November 13, 2001, it was over.[60]

As Afghan men, women, and children poured into the streets of Kabul to celebrate, Team 555 secured the U.S. embassy, which

Afghans Liberated

When the Taliban seized control of Afghanistan in 1996, they imposed harsh rules and laws they said were based on Islamic doctrine. Men were forced to grow beards. Women, no longer allowed to go to work, were required to cover themselves from head to toe by wearing a *burka* outside the home. Dancing, playing music, and flying kites were also forbidden because they were seen as frivolous activities by the Taliban. This all came to an end in Kabul on December 7, 2001, when the Northern Alliance, assisted by U.S. military forces, forced the Taliban out of the capital city. Joyous residents flooded the streets and danced to Indian music that had long been forbidden. Men shaved their beards and children made homemade kites and flew them over downtown. Girls were free to go back to school after a five-year ban. One Afghan girl expressed her happiness to a reporter for the *Christian Science Monitor*: "I cannot express my happiness to you," she said. "I can remember the day the Taliban came, and we went home in great sadness. But we are quite happy to return to school."

had been abandoned since the Taliban takeover in 1996. Later they opened the Kabul airfield, which quickly became a central staging area for international relief efforts. With Kabul fallen, Alliance-controlled territory in Afghanistan stretched from the Pakistan border in the east all the way to Herat in the west. The only remaining Taliban-held city in the north was Kunduz.

Siege at Kunduz

With the Taliban in disarray, many of the fighters retreated south, back to Kandahār to rally around their spiritual leader, Mullah Omar. U.S. fighter aircraft and Apache helicopters chased the retreating soldiers, targeting them relentlessly. Kunduz, meanwhile, was under fire by General Muhammad Daoud's Northern Alliance army. By mid-November more than five thousand Taliban and al-Qaeda were dug in and prepared to defend their last northern stronghold to the death. The race to take Kunduz was on. On November 22, with Dostum changing course and approaching fast from the west, Daoud launched an offensive against the city. U.S. Special Forces radioed for B-52 support as Daoud's forces attacked from the east. The next day the anti-Taliban forces had the city surrounded. Northern Alliance and Taliban commanders initiated negotiations for surrender, but those quickly broke down when some of the foreign fighters—mainly Chechens and Pakistanis—refused to surrender.

In the meantime, the Alliance armies of Dostum and Atta arrived, joining Daoud's

forces positioned around the city. For more than a week the Alliance had the city under siege, as diplomats and human rights organizations pleaded for the Alliance to achieve a peaceful surrender. In the end it was the threat of overwhelming U.S. air attacks that led to mass surrenders. Still, there were casualties and possibly some atrocities against Taliban prisoners by Dostum and his men. According to reports that surfaced later, up to 960 prisoners were packed into shipping crates and transported to Sheberghan prison near Dasht-e-Leili. Many of the captives died in transit and were allegedly buried in mass graves.

With Taliban surrender at Kunduz complete, the entire northern half of Afghanistan was under Northern Alliance control. Many of the Green Beret units began conducting humanitarian missions, including coordinating the flow of aid that was beginning to arrive from around the world. But others, along with CIA operatives and British Special Air Services (SAS), moved east and searched caves and other mountain hideouts for al-Qaeda fighters and clues that might lead to Osama bin Laden. There was strong suspicion that the terrorist leader had already slipped out of Afghanistan when it became clear the Taliban would fall. Secretary of State Powell, however, had his own opinion about the location of the world's most-wanted man:

I think he's still in Afghanistan simply because I have seen no intelligence or information to suggest he has left Afghan-

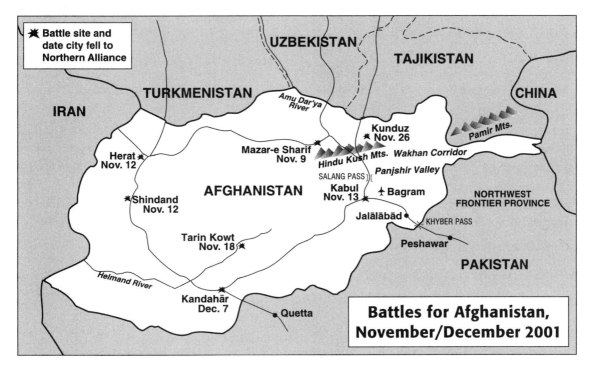

Battles for Afghanistan, November/December 2001

istan, and I don't know of any country in the region that would be very anxious to see him arrive. So I think he's still in Afghanistan, and it's getting harder for him to hide, as more and more territory is removed from Taliban control.[61]

Revolt at Qala-i-Jangi

Even with the capture of Kunduz, the northern part of Afghanistan remained unstable and dangerous. Furthermore, the difficult matter of captured Taliban and al-Qaeda soldiers remained to be solved. The Northern Alliance was ill prepared to handle unruly prisoners, so mistakes were bound to be made. On November 25 at Qala-i-Jangi, an ancient stone-walled prison

outside of Mazar-e Sharif, such mistakes demonstrated that northern Afghanistan still had the potential to slip back into brief periods of conflict.

Most of the six hundred prisoners at Qala-i-Jangi were Arab, Chechen, and Pakistani and were among al-Qaeda's most hardened fighters. With the aid of Northern Alliance guards, two CIA operatives, Johnny "Mike" Spann and David Tyson, were interrogating selected inmates. At some point several prisoners who had managed to smuggle some grenades inside the prison set them off. Six of the guards were killed in the explosion and the rest were overpowered. Spann was captured by the rebellious prisoners; Tyson escaped and radioed Special Forces for help.

American Taliban

John Walker Lindh, known as the "American Taliban" because he was among the captured Taliban fighters early in the war, was born near Washington, D.C., but moved to Marin County, California, at age ten. At age twelve, he became interested in Islam after watching the movie *Malcolm X*, in which the African American leader's conversion to Islam was portrayed. At around age sixteen Lindh became a devout Muslim and attended a mosque regularly. Under the names Suleyman al-Lindh and Suleyman al-Faris, he began a spiritual journey in July 1998 that took him to Yemen to study Arabic and Islam and to Pakistan, where he received military training. Beginning in June 2001, he spent seven weeks at al Farooq, an al-Qaeda training camp, where he met Osama bin Laden. After terrorists struck the United States on September 11, 2001, Lindh was deployed to the Taliban front lines. But when U.S. bombing began on October 7, he allegedly fled one hundred miles on foot to Kunduz, where he was captured and moved to the Qala-i-Jangi prison near Mazar-e Sharif. It was there that he was part of a prison revolt that claimed the life of CIA officer Johnny "Mike" Spann. On October 4, 2002, after receiving a twenty-year prison sentence for conspiring to kill Americans and providing support to terrorists, he addressed the court, saying, "I understand why so many Americans were angry when I was first discovered in Afghanistan. . . . Had I realized then what I know now . . . I . . . never would have joined them."

In short order, U.S. and British commandos surrounded the fortress and exchanged gunfire with the prisoners, who by now were well armed after raiding a weapons cache. The fighting was fierce at times and included a friendly fire incident in which a U.S. gunship accidentally fired on American troops. But by the end of the third day coalition forces had regrouped and forced most of the prisoners into submission. The last holdouts, more than eighty men, had retreated to an underground dungeon. Alliance soldiers flooded the basement with water and then threatened to pipe gasoline in and ignite it. Facing certain death, the prisoners surrendered. When the three-day uprising ended, more than four hundred prisoners and forty Northern Alliance soldiers were dead. CIA agent Spann had been killed in the siege, becoming the first American to die in combat in Operation Enduring Freedom.

In the aftermath of the uprising, questions were again raised about Northern Alliance atrocities against al-Qaeda prisoners, including deaths that were called suicides but which looked to some observers to have been executions. Justin Huggler, a reporter who visited Qala-i-Jangi one day after the revolt ended, was skeptical about the explanations put forth by the Alliance:

It was not the first time that we had heard of bin Laden's "foreigners" committing suicide rather than be taken alive. The Northern Alliance claimed that a group of around 60 of them jumped into a river and drowned themselves. Another group were found kneeling in positions of prayer, each with a single bullet wound from behind. A Northern Alliance commander alleged that one of them had killed all of the others in a suicide pact before turning the gun on himself. But there were always fears that the stories might have been invented to cover up Northern Alliance massacres of the foreign fighters.[62]

U.S. Marines Enter Afghanistan

After the uprising at Qala-i-Jangi and as the Northern Alliance's hold on northern Afghanistan grew firmer by the day, thousands of Taliban soldiers raced southward to regroup at Kandahār, one of the few remaining Taliban-held cities. A large American force was needed to cut off enemy escape routes and resupply columns to the southern city. Starting November 25, two U.S. Marine units totaling twelve hundred troops landed at a remote desert airstrip eighty miles southwest of Kandahār. Each marine unit was equipped with its own infantry, aircraft, and commandos. The presence of the two large marine forces marked a new phase in the campaign. For the first time, CENTCOM had a more conventional ground force to complement its overwhelming airpower. Rumsfeld explained why the marines were deployed in southern Afghanistan:

> The highways that connect the north and the south and the east/west in the southern part going towards Iran . . . or entrances from Iran or Pakistan can be interdicted from those locations. And it was decided that it would be helpful to have a base there from which a variety of things could be done rather than simply using people in and out of a Special Operations nature.[63]

The marines established a forward operating base, called Camp Rhino, which within days was teeming with Harrier jets, Cobra attack helicopters, light armored

A U.S. Marine mans his weapon. In November 2001, two U.S. Marine units were deployed to southern Afghanistan to cut off escape routes.

vehicles, 155-mm howitzer artillery, and other necessary equipment to fight a war in the desert wasteland of southern Afghanistan.

With Camp Rhino established as a major command-and-control center for operations in southern Afghanistan, several companies of marines set out into the desert to secure the base. They dug foxholes and stacked sandbags at various points around the perimeter to serve as forward positions from which to watch for enemy intrusion.

The marines' precautions soon proved necessary. A few days into the mission, Taliban armored vehicles attempted to probe the base after dark. The marines, in heavily armed Humvees and supported by Cobra attack helicopters, destroyed the enemy in short order. Meanwhile, other marine units fanned out in long-range "hunter-killer" missions, using Humvees, light armored vehicles, and Cobras. On one such operation in early December, marines encountered a column of Taliban tanks and armored personnel trying to break through a roadblock near Kandahār. The marines called in air and ground support and destroyed the column, killing seven Taliban soldiers. The marines then expanded their patrol areas and sometimes gave assistance to Special Operations forces fighting with local Pashtun opposition groups in the final push toward Kandahār.

Closing In on Kandahār

Back in mid-November the drive to Kandahār had accelerated when a force under a popular Pashtun leader, Hamid Karzai, with assistance from U.S. Special Forces A-Team 574, killed more than three hundred Taliban troops to capture the key southern city of Tarin Kowt, seventy miles north of Kandahār. Tarin Kowt sat in a valley at the intersection of two main highways, and Karzai's belief that its fall would speed the collapse of the Taliban in the south was confirmed. Karzai's men and his Special Forces attachment pressed southward, and on December 4 fought a fierce day-long battle with Taliban troops to take a key bridge at Sayed Alam-a-Kalay.

Shortly after their successful operation, however, just as Karzai's men were ready to resume their southward advance toward Kandahār, disaster struck. A two thousand-pound satellite-guided explosive, dropped from a B-52 bomber, was given the incorrect coordinates and exploded close to Karzai and his men and the Special Forces with them. The blast killed twenty-eight people, including three Green Berets. Karzai narrowly escaped with wounds to his face.

The errant American bomb delayed the assault on Kandahār, but by the next day, Karzai's anti-Taliban force and the team of Americans were positioned at the northern edge of the city. Another Pashtun tribal army, commanded by Gul Agha Sharzai, flanked the city to the south with another U.S. Special Forces team. With the city under siege, U.S. Marine hunter-killer teams patrolled the outskirts and attempted to intercept as many fleeing al-Qaeda and Taliban fighters as possible. But the area was large, and there

Camp X-Ray Controversy

In January 2002, the U.S. military began sending Taliban and al-Qaeda soldiers captured on the battlefield in Afghanistan to a temporary detention facility at Guantánamo Bay, the U.S. naval base in Cuba. The site, which became known as Camp X-Ray, became a source of controversy for the U.S. government. Although Department of Defense officials insisted the prisoners were being treated humanely and in accordance with the Geneva Conventions, images of kneeling prisoners with hands bound behind their backs sparked an international outcry. Adding to the furor was the Bush administration's refusal to afford the detainees prisoner of war status, which would have given them legal representation. Instead, the three hundred or so detainees were designated "illegal combatants," meaning they could be held indefinitely. To deflect claims of prisoner misconduct, the United States allowed visits by the International Red Cross, which found the detainees to be well fed and given access to regular shower and toilet facilities. A medical clinic was constructed on site to treat the injured. And due to blunt anger in the Muslim world, the Islamic prisoners were allowed to pray five times a day, as is customary in the Islamic faith, and given access to the Koran.

were many escape routes. Thousands of al-Qaeda and Taliban soldiers escaped to the mountains and some eventually crossed the border into Pakistan, where they found shelter among friendly Pashtun tribes. Mullah Omar, wearing common Afghan clothing, was reportedly spotted escaping on a motorcycle. Two days later, the two Pashtun forces, meeting little resistance, converged on Kandahār. Thousands of Afghans in the city celebrated their arrival.

As the anti-Taliban forces launched a fierce ground war, the coordination of air strikes by small teams of commandos was more successful than most military planners had thought possible. The Taliban collapse that had started at Mazar-e Sharif and ended in Kandahār was as stunning as it was convincing. But as the focus of battle turned toward al-Qaeda and bin Laden, the fight promised to take longer and become much more difficult.

Chapter 6

The Hunt for Osama bin Laden

The Taliban had been routed, fulfilling one of President George W. Bush's objectives. With the regime that had protected Osama bin Laden no longer in position to impede the search for al-Qaeda's leader, the hunt was on. That effort, however, would prove difficult and frustrating.

The Smoking Gun

In late November, the CIA had obtained a videotape of the terrorist leader talking with supporters about the terrorist attacks on America. U.S. authorities called it the "smoking gun," because it pointed to bin Laden's direct involvement in the attacks. The documented admission of guilt seemed to give the search for the terrorist leader a new impetus. But in spite of bin Laden's direct involvement in the attacks, Bush and his administration downplayed the importance of the al-Qaeda leader's capture in the war on terrorism. Americans, they said, should prepare for an extended battle against a dangerous and elusive enemy. Comments by the chairman of the Joint Chiefs of Staff, Richard Myers, were indicative of the Bush administration's long-term objectives: "I think what we have to tell the American public, is that we've got to be prepared for a long war. We've been saying this from the very beginning, that this is not going to be over if we get [Osama bin Laden], if we get a couple of his top lieutenants. We're talking about disabling the [al-Qaeda] network, and it's going to take some time."[64]

Privately, however, the Bush administration considered finding bin Laden of paramount importance. Although they believed he was clearly on the run, most of Bush's staff believed bin Laden to be an ongoing threat to the United States and its allies as long as he remained free.

Where bin Laden might be, however, was a matter of conjecture. Expecting bin Laden to have been hiding in Kandahār with Mullah Omar, American intelligence operatives had focused their search for him there. But in late November, before Kandahār fell, the CIA became convinced that he and a cadre of his loyal al-Qaeda followers were in the White Mountains, along the Afghan-Pakistan border. His precise location was unknown, but all signs pointed to Tora Bora, a remote area riddled with natural caves that had been used by the mujahideen during the Soviet occupation of Afghanistan.

Tora Bora

Any assault on Tora Bora would be arduous. During their ten-year occupation, the Soviets had not managed to root out the mujahideen at the mountain hideout. Now the caves were even more secure, after bin Laden had financed their expansion and reinforcement in the 1990s. Tunnels were believed to bore more than one hundred feet underground, and large caches of weapons were thought to

have been placed throughout the complex. The U.S. plan for attacking Tora Bora was again to use a massive bombing campaign as Special Forces assisted anti-Taliban fighters on the ground. The goal was to destroy the cave sanctuaries and drive the Taliban and al-Qaeda high into the mountains, where the Pakistan army would intercept anyone trying to escape across the border.

The assault began on November 30 as the Green Berets and Afghan troops mounted a three-pronged attack up the western face of the mountain, putting them in closer position to many of the cave entrances. Over a two-week period allied warplanes fired "cave buster" smart bombs that flew into the entrances and detonated there. The resulting fireball consumed enormous amounts of oxygen, creating a powerful vacuum, which had devastating consequences for anyone inside. Laser-guided bombs were

The Myth of Tora Bora

In the buildup to the battle at Tora Bora in December 2001, the news media reported extensively on an elaborate underground bunker complex deep in the White Mountains of eastern Afghanistan. According to those reports, after the Soviet Union invaded Afghanistan in 1979, the CIA, and later Osama bin Laden, had the underground channels expanded and reinforced. The military bunkers were invaluable to the mujahideen, who used them as hideouts and staging grounds for guerrilla attacks on the Soviet troops. The complex was now said to hold a command-and-control center, a high-tech communication complex, elaborate sleeping quarters, and more. A November 26, 2001, article in the *New York Times* examined the

Tora Bora complex and featured a former Russian soldier who claimed to have been inside Tora Bora. He described a vast, multitiered underground fortress complete with "a bakery, a hotel with overstuffed furniture, a hospital with an ultrasound machine, a library, a mosque, weapons of every imaginable stripe." Only when coalition soldiers entered the bombed-out caves after the fighting stopped did U.S. soldiers find out the truth about Tora Bora. Most of the caves were capable of holding no more than a few men. There were small rooms for sleeping, some of them ventilated, along with crevices dug into the side of the mountain where weapons were stored. The soldiers found none of the high-tech gadgetry they had expected.

also fired at cave entrances, producing a massive concussion that ripped through the twisting chasms. The air force also dropped daisy cutter bombs, collapsing caves and killing anyone within its large blast radius, aboveground or below. By December 13, battered al-Qaeda forces were ready to negotiate a surrender. But U.S. commandos sensed secret deals were also being made between al-Qaeda and Northern Alliance commanders. As a result, Americans pressured their Afghan partners to renew their attacks.

For Pashtun commanders, figuring heavily into the manhunt was a $25 million reward for bin Laden's capture, but Moore reveals why the high-dollar prize was not an effective way to entice the lower-ranking foot soldiers to put forth their best efforts in the search:

> The soldiers knew that even if they had bin Laden in the back of their Toyota and tied up in barbed wire, it would not matter—they would never see one dime of the money because it would all go to big commanders and politicians. In one way it was even worse: Afghans had virtually no understanding of what $25 million meant. Exactly how many donkeys, camels, or Toyota Land Cruisers did that add up to? That was the way Afghans

A Northern Alliance tank fires at al-Qaeda fighters hiding in Tora Bora's White Mountains.

counted wealth and power—by live-stock, Land Cruisers, and the number of soldiers you could feed.[65]

The Trail Runs Cold

On December 16, the searchers thought they finally had located bin Laden, whose short-range radio commands to his soldiers had been intercepted. Bin Laden, it appeared, was still in Tora Bora, but he was preparing to leave. A massive search ensued, with a two-man sniper team quickly flown in to set up an ambush where bin Laden was believed to be heading. There, they waited with guns at the ready. Less than thirty-six hours later, the Green Berets had a positive fix on a man who appeared to be bin Laden. The man many people believe was bin Laden escaped, however. Ready to fire their weapons, the two commandos were told to stand down because they were outnumbered, making the mission too risky.

As the fighting tailed off at Tora Bora, the commandos' new mission was to search caves, accompanied by CIA operatives, for any information that would provide clues about the workings of the al-Qaeda network or indicate the whereabouts of bin Laden. Though many of the caves had been destroyed in the bombing campaign and others turned out to be empty, some provided a wealth of intelligence. On January 9, 2002, for example, a team of Special Forces captured two senior al-Qaeda members and twelve of their men hiding inside a cave. Commandos also found computers, documents, and manuals there. Analysis of these materials in turn led to the arrest of al-Qaeda terrorists in other countries, including a large network in Singapore and Malaysia. Biological and chemical weapons specialists conducted cave searches to learn whether bin Laden's network had acquired these items, but found no traces of either type of weapon. Army forensic experts also entered the caves to search for bin Laden's body, on the chance he had been killed in the bombing. These searches likewise were dead ends.

In the days and weeks following the Tora Bora operation, military analysts scrutinized the U.S. decision not to commit more ground troops to the battle at Tora Bora. The analysts asserted that America's reliance on Afghan fighters had allowed the enemy to escape simply because the Alliance forces were too inexperienced for such a massive operation. More disturbing, though, were the alleged secret deals taking place that allowed al-Qaeda fighters—and possibly even bin Laden himself—to escape. Ultimately, putting more U.S. troops on the ground and taking the fight to the enemy would have been the preferred method, according to Charles Heyman, British editor of *Jane's World Armies*:

The initial stages of the war in Afghanistan were superbly executed, especially the air strikes that destroyed the Taliban on the ground. But after that, there were never enough forces on the ground. And if you don't have enough forces on the ground, you can't dictate events on the ground. That is one of the reasons so many escaped.[66]

President Bush, however, supported U.S. commanders' conduct of the war. He gave this positive assessment of the ongoing search for the al-Qaeda leader:

[Bin Laden is] on the run, if he's running at all. . . . We don't know whether he's in a cave with the door shut or a cave with the door open; we just don't know. There's all kinds of reports and all kinds of speculation, but one thing we know is that he's not in charge of Afghanistan anymore . . . we know that for certain. And we also know that we're on the hunt, and he knows that we're on the hunt. And I like our position better than his.[67]

Operation Anaconda

Beyond the search for Osama bin Laden and Mullah Omar, the United States and its allies had to deal with ongoing instability in Afghanistan. For example, in February 2002, al-Qaeda and Taliban fighters were found to be regrouping in the Shah-i-Kot valley between the Afghan villages of Gardez and Khost, near the Pakistani border. The predominantly Arab and Chechen fighters were preparing to cross into Pakistan, where they were believed to be attempting to rally other Afghans in the re-gion for a new jihad against the Americans and their allies. It was rumored that Mullah Omar had offered a $50,000 reward for the death of any foreigner, including journalists and humanitarian aid workers. The Taliban still clearly presented a threat to the fragile peace process that was just underway in Afghanistan.

In response to such threats, in late February, coalition forces prepared to launch Operation Anaconda, so called because the goal was to surround enemy fighters with a heavy concentration of troops and "squeeze" them toward higher ground as U.S. warplanes dropped an array of ordnance. The war at this point clearly became an international effort as coalition partners taking part in the operation included Australia, Canada, Denmark, France, Germany, and Norway, as well as U.S. and Afghan forces. The importance of the operation became clear when nearly fifteen hundred U.S. ground troops took a leading role in combat. U.S. troops were made up of soldiers mainly from the army's 10th Mountain Division and 101st Airborne.

The operation began when allied forces took off from Bagram Air Base in the pre-dawn hours of March 2. Coalition forces swept into the Shah-i-Kot valley near Gardez. Their helicopters quickly came under attack by al-Qaeda rocket-propelled grenades. When the U.S. soldiers hit the ground, they found themselves engaged in some of the heaviest combat of the war. The soldiers scratched for every inch of territory in the mountain terrain, exchanging fierce gun-

Mistakes of War

Friendly fire incidents and civilian casualties are an inevitable part of war, and Operation Enduring Freedom had its share of both. On the night of April 17, 2002, Canadian troops were conducting live-fire exercises in southern Afghanistan when they were mistaken for Taliban soldiers by two U.S. Navy F-16 fighter pilots, Maj. Harry Schmidt and Maj. William Umbach. Amid confusion Schmidt dropped a five-hundred-pound laser-guided bomb directly on top of the Canadian allies, killing four soldiers. The mishap drew widespread anger in Canada and put a strain on relations between the two nations. When a joint U.S.-Canadian investigation concluded that the pilots were at fault, the U.S. Air Force initially brought involuntary manslaughter charges against them. The charges against Umbach were eventually dropped, but Schmidt, after refusing to accept lesser charges offered by the air force, faced a possible court-martial and prison sentence.

Another controversial mistake of war happened on July 1, 2002, when a U.S. Air Force AC-130 gunship flying over southern Afghanistan about one hundred miles north of Kandahār reportedly came under hostile gunfire. The AC-130 pilot returned fire, but the shooters on the ground were not members of the Taliban or al-Qaeda; they instead turned out to be Afghan civilians at a prewedding party who were allegedly firing their guns into the air in celebration. Afghan officials claimed 48 people were killed and 117 others injured, though the numbers were not confirmed. Among the wounded was Haji Mohammed Anwar, a friend of President Hamid Karzai. Ironically, Karzai had been worried about the possibility of this kind of mistake, telling an Associated Press reporter one week earlier, "I will definitely want the Afghan civilians, the Afghan villages to be immune from accidental damage. To be sure that they do not receive accidental firing at them. To make sure that our women and children and villages don't suffer."

fire with the highly trained and surprisingly accurate al-Qaeda marksmen. The Americans called for air support from Apache and Cobra attack helicopters and AC-130 gunships. Air Force F-15s and Navy F-14s also arrived to take out enemy troops.

As in earlier operations, some casualties were attributable to friendly fire. An AC-130 gunship providing close air support to Afghan troops and their U.S. Special Forces advisers mistook them for al-Qaeda combatants. One Green Beret and three Afghan fighters were killed, while two Green Berets and more than twenty Afghans were wounded. Allied forces were ordered to pull back toward Gardez, because the situation was too unstable.

Taliban and al-Qaeda resistance continued, sometimes inflicting significant casualties. For example, before dawn on March 4, a team of navy SEALs in an MH-47 helicopter came under attack by al-Qaeda snipers. The helicopter was struck, and as its pilot fought for control of the airship a SEAL fell out of the open ramp in the back. Before the team could rescue their comrade, he was shot at point-blank range by enemy fighters, a scene captured on video by a UAV Predator drone circling high above the battlefield. A second crew, unaware that the SEAL was dead, raced toward the scene in their helicopter, but it too was hit by enemy fire and crash-landed. One man died instantly and four others were killed in the ensuing gunfight with al-Qaeda soldiers. The seven fatalities on that day were the largest U.S. loss of life in a single engagement to that point in the war.

"Unqualified and Absolute Success"

By the fourth day of Operation Anaconda, warplanes were delivering relentless strikes against al-Qaeda positions, with French Mirage 200 jet aircraft and U.S. Air Force ground support A-10 Thunderbolts entering the air campaign for the first time. Due to the A-10s' reinforced cockpits, pilots were able to aim their munitions into caves from close range, making them a valuable

asset in this fierce and ongoing battle. The attack planes were believed to have killed some two hundred fighters during Operation Anaconda alone. But when the opposition remained firmly dug in even after the massive air assault, another three hundred U.S. soldiers were called into battle to increase the pressure. The battle raged on all sides of the mountain, with more and more American soldiers inserted daily. Af-

A U.S. soldier watches for enemy movement during Operation Anaconda. The operation resulted in heavy casualties for the Taliban and al-Qaeda.

ter ten days of targeted air strikes and heavy pressure from the ground force, al-Qaeda and Taliban troops finally showed signs of breaking. Any attempts to escape to the east were thwarted by Canadian snipers blocking mountain passes leading into Pakistan. Still, many of the al-Qaeda fighters escaped by slipping into small villages, where anti-American sentiment was strong, and they could blend in with the civilian population.

Fighting continued for several days before Centcom declared the mission complete. Two weeks of intensive air bombing and ground combat had left seven hundred al-Qaeda and Taliban fighters dead. The number of U.S. casualties was nowhere near as high—eight dead and forty-nine wounded. General Franks visited the troops at Bagram Air Base and awarded Purple Hearts and medals of valor to the wounded Americans. He also took time to address the troops after their mission. In his remarks Franks noted the continuing dangers:

> What I have seen leads me to believe this operation was an unqualified and absolute success, not only from all the American and coalition forces involved but also from all the Afghans involved. . . . Does the possibility exist for another group of foreign fighters inside Afghanistan such as we found in the Shah-i-Kot area? Yes, I believe it's possible for fighters to group in various places. I think that is why we have to be careful to say this is not over. One should suspect the oper-

ations will continue because, yes, there's a possibility for some [al-Qaeda] forces to maybe regroup and perhaps enemy forces we've not yet found the location of.[68]

Search and Destroy

With the end of Operation Anaconda, a new strategy emerged. Coalition forces now began conducting a series of small search-and-destroy missions, largely independent of their Afghan allies. The objective was to search for al-Qaeda and Taliban troops, capture and/or destroy al-Qaeda weapons, and stabilize the area so it would be safe for workers when humanitarian operations began. The search-and-destroy missions took soldiers anywhere in the country where terrorists were suspected to be hiding, but most of the action concentrated in the eastern mountains near the Afghan-Pakistan border.

These smaller-scale missions encountered little or no resistance, yet they could be dangerous. Starting on April 15, Operation Mountain Lion took place in the Gardez and Khost regions near the Pakistan border, the battleground in which Operation Anaconda was fought. Units from a battalion of the army's 187th Infantry and 101st Airborne Division fanned out and, armed with assault rifles, scoured the Zawahkili cave complex and other sensitive areas. Although no fighting took place in this mission, four U.S. soldiers were killed when an al-Qaeda rocket exploded as they were destroying a large cache of weapons. Then, starting in early May, British forces, which had entered Afghanistan one month earlier, took the leading role in a similar search-and-destroy mission called Operation Snipe. One thousand Royal Marine commandos supported by Royal Air Force (RAF) Chinook helicopters entered southeastern Afghanistan, territory that had not yet been searched by coalition forces. Once again the commandos did not encounter any resistance but did find a major cave network filled with mortars, antitank guns, rocket-propelled grenades, small arms, and antiaircraft ammunition. Demolition experts wired the caves with explosives and detonated them, destroying the complexes and the weapons inside.

Operation Mountain Sweep followed in mid-August 2002, with more than two thousand coalition troops including units from the 82nd Airborne Division and Rangers taking part in the eight-day operation. The mission was concentrated in and around the southeastern Afghan villages of Dormat and Narizah, former al-Qaeda and Taliban strongholds. Coalition forces mounted combat air assault missions, but, like previous search-and-destroy missions, they encountered no main force al-Qaeda and Taliban fighters. The mission was considered a success, however, when troops found five separate weapons caches and a wealth of Taliban documents. U.S. Army commander in Afghanistan Lieutenant General Dan K. McNeill noted that the search-and-destroy missions were having the desired effect:

U.S. soldiers search for Taliban and al-Qaeda fighters along Afghanistan's eastern border.

We are doing things each day that make it harder and harder for the terrorists not only to operate but to survive. We're continuing to chip away at the [al-Qaeda] organization. We don't have to find [bin Laden] because we are going to shut down his terrorist apparatus. . . . We haven't won, but we're winning.[69]

Evaluating the War

As the one-year mark of fighting the war against terrorism in Afghanistan approached, military analysts began assessing the successes and failures of the campaign. Most notable was the swift downfall of the Taliban after its initial heavy resistance. Between three thousand and four thousand Taliban troops were killed in action, and approximately seven thousand were taken prisoner. By contrast the United States lost fewer than fifty soldiers, many of whom died in helicopter accidents and friendly fire incidents. Whether the main objective of the war—destroying al-Qaeda's ability to function—had been attained was not so easy to determine. On one hand, al-Qaeda had not mounted new attacks on the United States or its allies since the campaign had started. However, bin Laden's fate remained unknown. Some people believed he had died inside the caves of Tora Bora during the massive U.S. bombing. But many others believed he had escaped, and until he could be captured, he would be considered a threat to America and its allies. His haven for training terrorists had been eliminated, but many of his secret al-Qaeda cells remained in place in the Middle East and elsewhere.

On the one-year anniversary of Operation Enduring Freedom, Richard Myers addressed the troops, not letting the disappointment surrounding the failure to learn bin Laden's fate keep him from lauding the

Al-Jazeera: Voice of the Arabs

In much of the Arab world, where the media is under tight state control, the satellite television station Al-Jazeera is considered an independent and often outspoken source of news. The Qatar-based network started broadcasting in 1996 and modeled itself after CNN both in style and format. Although the network claimed 35 million viewers during Operation Enduring Freedom, its frank views on the war won few fans in the Bush administration. U.S. officials particularly disliked what they perceived as an anti-American bias in some of its reporting. For example, Al-Jazeera featured exclusive footage of bin Laden as well as recorded interviews or taped messages. Al-Jazeera frequently also showed Afghan homes and property allegedly damaged by U.S. and coalition forces. Indeed, the images angered the Muslim world, where anger rose with each civilian casualty. To counter Al-Jazeera's influence in the region, the United States launched an Arab radio station called Radio Sawa, or "Radio Together." In an effort to win the hearts and minds of the Arab youth, who make up 60 percent of the population in the region, Radio Sawa features a mix of American and Arab pop music. It also broadcasts regular news and headline segments that counter the anti-American spin that is frequently put on the news in the Middle East. Norman Pattiz, Radio Sawa's creator, told the U.S. Senate's Committee on Foreign Relations,

When President Bush, in his October 2001 speech to the Nation, after the tragic events of 9/11, asked in so many words why do they hate us, I believe the answer is because they don't know us. All they hear about America and Americans comes from sources that are invested in not presenting a truthful picture of the United States—and the world. Radio Sawa is the first step, presenting our people and policies accurately from our own lips.

efforts of the military men and women who fought extraordinarily well in Afghanistan:

A year ago at this time, few predicted the speed or the effectiveness with which we would eliminate the major terrorist haven in Afghanistan. It was a landlocked country. We had no military bases in the vicinity. We had no major war plan to remove the Taliban from power. Then, twenty-seven days after the terrorists struck our nation, this joint team unleashed a powerful and lethal campaign. Two months later, our men and women, in concert with our allies and friends, freed Afghanistan. . . . This campaign has been one for the record books. It included the deepest amphibious operation in our Marine Corps history—over 400 miles into hostile territory. It included the highest elevation that our soldiers fought a pitched battle—at 10,000 feet above sea level. It included the longest combat sortie on record for our Air Force—44 hours in length. Most significant of all, it entailed the fewest warcombatant injuries and the least collateral damage of any major military operation in history.[70]

In October 2002 an audiotape purportedly of bin Laden's voice was broadcast by Al-Jazeera. In the tape he warned Americans that al-Qaeda was preparing for future attacks on the United States. But some analysts doubted the tape was a recent recording, since it contained no references to events subsequent to the assault on Tora Bora. However, a month later, Al-Jazeera broadcast another bin Laden audiotape; this time he praised specific attacks, including one carried out in October in which Chechen rebels took a theater audience hostage in Moscow. Clearly, the most wanted man in the world had survived the war in Afghanistan.

Chapter 7

The Struggle for Peace

As U.S. military involvement in Afghanistan passed the one-year mark, Pentagon officials attempted to shift the focus away from military combat and toward peacekeeping and reconstruction efforts in the war-ravaged nation. But pockets of resistance remained along the southeastern Afghan border. Taliban and al-Qaeda fighters who had fled to the mountains there in late 2001 and early 2002 were increasing their harassing, guerrilla-style attacks on U.S. and coalition forces. The Taliban rebels desired a return to power, and they threatened to diminish the military success achieved by the coalition in the campaign. Afghanistan clearly remained a dangerous and unstable nation, and "winning the peace" would require a determined effort.

The Loya Jirga

When the Taliban was removed from power in December 2001, the coalition quickly established a framework for a tran-

sitional Afghan government. Hamid Karzai, the Pashtun leader who had fought alongside U.S. commandos in the charge to take Kandahār, was selected as chairman of the provisional government. Although some Afghans saw the pro-Western Karzai as an American-installed puppet leader, most Afghans admired him and pinned their hopes on his ability to bring lasting peace to the country for the first time in decades. The interim government lasted six months, providing the coalition enough time to stabilize Kabul, even as fierce fighting between allied forces and Taliban and al-Qaeda rebels was still taking place along the Afghan-Pakistan border.

Then, in June 2002, the Loya Jirga, an assembly of 1,550 Afghan delegates, convened in the capital city to elect a new leader of a transitional government body. While the Bush administration strongly supported Karzai's continuing role as head of the fragile Afghan government, many Afghans favored the return of Muhammad Zahir Shah, the former king. Shah had fled to Italy in 1973 when the Soviet-backed Communists overthrew his government, and his return was widely believed to be the best way to unite the nation. But Tajiks in the Loya Jirga were against the Pashtun former king leading Afghanistan, and they became locked in a bitter power struggle with Pashtun representatives. Some observers believe that with ethnic tension threatening to disrupt the proceedings and a potential new government, the United States intervened and quietly pressured the king not to accept the role. Although Secretary of State Powell denied any U.S. influence, the former king eventually declined to be considered for leadership in the new government.

After nine days of bitter argument and impassioned speeches, the Loya Jirga voted Karzai interim president of the Transitional

Hamid Karzai: Natural Leader

Hamid Karzai was born in Kandahār, Afghanistan, on December 24, 1957. He is a member of the Popolzai tribe, a branch of the Durrani clan that had traditionally produced Afghanistan's kings when the nation was ruled by a monarchy. Leadership has long been a quality of the Karzai family. Karzai's father was the chieftain of the Popolzai tribe and a former senator in the Afghan parliament. Hamid Karzai's leadership skills became evident after the Soviet Union invaded Afghanistan. Attending university and studying political science in India at the time, he eventually relocated to Pakistan and became the director of operations in the Afghan National Liberation Front, an organization that aided the mujahideen in their fight against the Soviets. After the Soviets pulled out of Afghanistan, Karzai entered the national political stage, serving as deputy foreign minister from 1992 to 1994.

The Taliban's rise in Afghanistan led to Karzai's exile to Quetta, Pakistan. There he became chief of the Popolzai tribe after his father's assassination in 1999. In October 2001, after the United States began air strikes in Afghanistan, he slipped back into the country and assembled a Pashtun militia to fight the Taliban in southern Afghanistan. Karzai's men, with assistance from U.S. Special Forces, helped bring about the Taliban's defeat in Kandahār in early December.

Hamid Karzai speaks to reporters in Kabul.

Authority, to serve until June 2004, when free elections would be held. After his selection he vowed to lead an independent and Islamic government and stated he would govern in a way few Afghans had before him. "No bribery, no ethnic parties, no guns and no warlords," he proclaimed. "And if I don't fulfill this promise to the people, tell me, because then I swear I will resign."[71]

Even with the hope for peace that a strong national government offered, violent elements of Afghanistan's former regime continued to cause trouble. Haji Abdul Qadir, Afghan vice president and a former commander in the Northern Alliance that had helped to topple the Taliban, was assassinated by pro-Taliban gunmen after less than one month in office. Two months later Karzai was also the target of an attempt on his life by Taliban sympathizers but narrowly escaped when his U.S. Special Forces bodyguard gunned down the would-be assassin. The assassination attempt followed a violent explosion in Kabul that killed almost 30 people and wounded 150 more. Again al-Qaeda and Taliban sympathizers were blamed for the attacks.

Trouble on the Border

Yet, as Operation Enduring Freedom passed the one-year mark, American military planners, in anticipation of war in Iraq, began shifting military aircraft and ships away from Afghanistan and closer to the Middle East. The USS *Abraham Lincoln*—the last aircraft carrier to remain in the Afghan theater—had already departed for the Persian Gulf

in September. But the military campaign in Afghanistan would soon prove to be far from over. Perhaps sensing an enemy losing focus in Afghanistan, remnants of al-Qaeda and Taliban fighters were becoming more active than they had been in months. For example, in mid-November, American forces engaged in two separate firefights. Small Afghan rebel forces fired rockets, mortar rounds, and rocket-propelled grenades at ground troops in eastern Afghanistan near Gardez and Lwara. After an A-10 Thunderbolt and a Marine AV-8 Harrier jet engaged the enemy, Eighty-second Airborne paratroopers exchanged gunfire and mortar rounds with the Afghan rebels until several fighters were killed and the rest slipped back into their mountain hideouts. The attacks were believed to be the work of Gulbuddin Hekmatyar, a former Afghan mujahideen who had fought against the Soviets in the 1980s. The CIA believed Hekmatyar was joining forces with his old enemy, Mullah Omar, to rally Taliban troops along the Pakistan border. Their goal was to create resentment and ultimately rebellion among common Afghans by casting the United States and its coalition partners as occupiers.

To better respond to the emerging threat of guerrilla attacks like those near Gardez and Lwara, the U.S. military brought in powerful 105-mm mobile howitzers—the first heavy artillery used in the Afghan campaign—to provide cover for ground troops. The Americans also set up several small military outposts along the Pakistani border to serve as bases. Coalition troops

used the bases for the continuing search for Taliban and al-Qaeda holdouts. Military analysts saw the introduction of heavy artillery and the military bases as a sign that the United States was preparing to keep a long-term presence in the troubled nation.

A New Day for Afghans?

Many in the Bush administration believed that Afghanistan could not establish a stable government until attacks of the sort mounted by Hekmatyar were ended. A plan was put in place to build a seventy-thousand-strong Afghan national army to replace the warlord-controlled militias in the provinces, who were by then once again fighting not

Members of the Afghan army salute. The United States played a crucial role in outfitting and training the new recruits.

only the American coalition but also one another. The aim was to decrease tribal conflict and make the country less likely to slip back into a civil war. The United States took a leading role in training the Afghan army, particularly in techniques of counterterrorism. But most military experts agreed it would be years before the army would be able to provide true security for all Afghans. For the next several years the role of stabilizing Kabul and other cities would be the responsibility of an eight-thousand-member international peacekeeping force from Denmark, Germany, Scotland, Turkey, and others willing to commit troops to the cause. But Defense Secretary Rumsfeld was not convinced that a large security force was the key to lasting peace in the war-torn nation:

> The reality is that you could stick a half a million troops from 20 countries into Afghanistan, and you wouldn't necessarily improve the security circumstance, as long as you've got Taliban and al-Qaida in Pakistan and Iran and porous borders. What has to be done is not to dramatically increase the number of security people, in my view, but the government has to find its sea legs. And it has to develop the confidence. . . . People have to develop confidence in that government that that government is delivering for them and making their lives better. And that means you've got to focus on the humanitarian side. You simply have to focus on the civil works side. And people have to develop a stake in that country and in that government.[72]

The U.S.-led coalition attempted to do exactly what Rumsfeld suggested in the earliest days after the Taliban were driven from power. The U.S. Combined Joint Civil-Military Operations Task Force took a leading role in the reconstruction and humanitarian aid efforts in Afghanistan. The task force began public works projects such as reconstructing hospitals, medical clinics, and schools. And medical personnel treated thousands of Afghan patients, while veterinarians examined and vaccinated livestock belonging to Afghan farmers and nomads. U.S. troops in Afghanistan also took time for more lighthearted activities designed to foster goodwill. Members of the Ninety-sixth Civil Affairs Battalion, for example, taught Afghan children how to play baseball, and the sport became an instant favorite.

But perhaps most important was the slow but steady return of millions of Afghan refugees who had fled the continued violence in the country. With the Taliban confined mainly to southeastern Afghanistan, the displaced Afghans, who had been living in refugee camps in Iran, Pakistan, Uzbekistan, and elsewhere, crossed the border and made the long journey back home. This fact more than any other seemed to suggest that Afghanistan was beginning to emerge from the dark shadows of war.

In Kabul the situation seemed equally hopeful as people were finally adjusting to life without the fear and oppression they had grown accustomed to after five years of living under harsh Taliban rule. *National Geographic* reporter Edward Girardet gave this promising account of the capital city's postwar atmosphere:

> Kabul is finally beginning to live again. The bazaars throng with merchants, returned refugees, former fighters, and farmers. Music blares from packed *chaikhane*, or teahouses, many of which sprout satellite dishes for television sets perpetually tuned, it seems, to the

highly popular Indian movie or music channels previously banned under the Taliban. Shop stalls brim with imported goods ranging from Russian refrigerators and tires to Chinese teapots, as well as the latest CDs and DVDs at black market rates of barely a dollar each. On the outskirts of town, food markets overflow with produce, while nomads bring in their camels, sheep, and goats for sale. Perhaps the most encouraging sign of the city's rebirth is the recent opening of its schools, particularly the girls' schools, closed under the Taliban.[73]

Taliban Resurgence

While many parts of the country showed great hope for peace, and humanitarian missions were being carried out daily, the troublesome southeastern border region, particularly the area around Kandahār, remained a concern for U.S. military forces. On January 28, 2003, a quick-reaction force of U.S. commandos, Eighty-second Airborne Division, along with select members of the newly formed Afghan army, launched Operation Mongoose after learning that rebels were holed up in caves in the Adi Gahr Mountains, near the village of Spinboldak. As the Americans and their Afghan allies approached in Apache attack helicopters, they came under attack by rocket-propelled grenades and small arms fire. Within minutes the troops were on the ground and calling in air support, including U.S. B-1 bombers and Norwegian F-16 fighters. Fierce gunfights between the troops and

Afghan rebels lasted through the night. Coalition aircraft targeted the cave hideouts with laser-guided munitions while helicopters and gunships unleashed round after round of lethal rocket and cannon fire. By the next morning at least eighteen Taliban rebels were dead. The brief but fierce combat was the heaviest fighting in Afghanistan since Operation Anaconda had ended nearly one year earlier. The mission lasted into early February, with troops searching more than fifty caves for enemy combatants. No fighters were found alive, but searchers found large quantities of food and blankets and large caches of rockets and artillery. Once the caves were cleared, commandos marked the entrances with their laser-markers, and smart bombs dropped from aircraft sealed the caves.

Determined to keep the enemy from regrouping, the coalition expanded the hunt for al-Qaeda and Taliban fugitives along the Afghan border. Five hundred troops fanned out and continued the search-and-destroy operations, detaining enemy combatants and recovering weapons of all kinds, including bomb-making materials, artillery rounds, rocket launchers, mines, and machine guns. By forcing the Taliban rebels farther into the mountains and destroying their weapons, the United States and its allies were attempting to diminish the chances of the enemy attacking, thereby giving the fledgling Afghan government more time to continue stabilizing the nation. But the Taliban were patient. They would likely stay hidden in their mountain enclaves, waiting for another chance to emerge and attack once again.

New Hope for Afghan Women

Women have traditionally held a secondary role in Afghanistan's male-dominated society. But when the Taliban regime came to power in the mid-1990s, basic rights for women eroded altogether. They were not allowed to work, go to school, or appear outside the home without the company of a man or without the all-concealing *burka*. After the U.S.-led coalition toppled the Taliban regime, women's rights were gradually restored. As millions of displaced women and children returned home from refugee camps, the United States and the Afghan government joined efforts to create the U.S.-Afghan Women's Council. Education and job training, access to health care, and political participation were several of the council's objectives to ensure women played an active role in Afghan society. These efforts have yielded positive results. Women have returned to work. Education is now available to girls and women. And women can leave their homes alone without fear of punishment. But with remnants of the Taliban regime surfacing in the south and increased fighting among warlords around the country, these important gains remain fragile and threaten to unravel.

A group of Afghan girls attends school for the first time since the Taliban seized power.

A War on Two Fronts

The threat the Taliban posed was real. With signs pointing to all-out war between the United States and Iraq, Hamid Karzai became concerned that the United States would assume a lesser role in Afghanistan, making a Taliban resurgence even more likely. Karzai, in Washington, D.C., in late February 2003 to ensure continued support for his country, told President Bush:

> Don't forget us if [war against] Iraq happens. If you reduce the attention because of Iraq . . . and if you leave the whole thing to us to fight again, it will be repeating the mistake the United States made during the Soviet occupation. Once the Soviets left, the Americans left. The consequence of that was what you saw in Afghanistan and in the United States and in the rest of the world. . . . The fight against terrorism is not completed. You have to see them totally defeated and gone before we can presume that Afghanistan is now out of the woods. . . . We are nearly at the end of the forest, [but] not outside of it.[74]

Insisting the United States was still committed to Afghanistan, U.S. officials pointed to the fact that the number of eight thousand or so American troops had not decreased over the last year. "The United States is capable of doing more than one thing at a time," said Zalmay Khalilzad, special U.S. envoy to Afghanistan. "The resources required for Afghanistan in its entirety . . . we are committed to delivering on, no matter what happens in Iraq."[75]

The U.S. stuck to that promise. On March 20, 2003, the United States launched Tomahawk cruise missiles against Iraq to start Operation Iraqi Freedom. Fifteen minutes after the missiles struck their target, U.S.-led forces in Afghanistan launched Operation Valiant Strike, a predawn offensive aimed at searching villages and cave complexes east of Kandahār for suspected Taliban and hidden weapons. Prompted by intercepted radio transmissions indicating the possibility of terrorist hideouts in three small villages in the Sami Ghar Mountains, approximately one thousand U.S. troops took off in Chinook and Black Hawk helicopters and Apache gunships. The troops discovered a stash of hidden Taliban weapons, including rifles, machine guns, rockets, and mortar rounds in addition to recruiting documents and other propaganda. The lightning raid followed in the pattern of most search-and-destroy missions over the last twelve months in Afghanistan. "It's a good mission," said an army medic participating in Valiant Strike. "We have these guys on the run. We've captured quite a few guys and the rest are on the run so they don't have any time to plan any missions."[76]

Al-Qaeda Renews Attacks

Serving as additional proof that the United States was committed to continuing the war on terrorism in the Afghan region was the apprehension of a top lieutenant in the al-Qaeda network. In early March, Pakistani ISI

U.S. soldiers inspect weapons found in a mountain village in southern Afghanistan.

operatives, working with the CIA, captured Khalid Sheikh Mohammed in Pakistan. According to U.S. officials, his capture was one of the most important developments thus far in the war against terrorism. Mohammed was believed to be number three in the al-Qaeda network and the alleged mastermind behind the September 11 terrorist attacks. He was also believed to be planning new terrorist attacks against the United States in the days leading up to his arrest. White House press secretary Ari Fleischer renewed Bush's warning to the terrorists: "The president's message to all al-Qaeda, whether it's Osama bin Laden or any of his other lieutenants . . . is there is no place to hide. They will be caught whatever length of time it takes."[77]

Later that month it appeared as though the net was closing on bin Laden. The ISI and CIA purportedly obtained from Mohammed intelligence on bin Laden, including details about a December 2002 meeting between the two men. Using the new information, intelligence operatives were allegedly hot on bin Laden's trail but, as had often proved to be the case with the international terrorist, he eluded capture. Soon after that an audiotape of bin Laden's voice was heard calling for more Muslim martyrdom operations. In the tape he gave the following command:

Officials linked Osama bin Laden to several bombings in early 2003, including this one at a restaurant in Morocco.

True Muslims should act, incite and mobilize the nation in such great events . . . in order to break free from the slavery of these tyrannic and apostate regimes enslaved by America. Among regions ready for liberation are Jordan, Morocco, Nigeria, the country of the two shrines (Saudi Arabia), Yemen and Pakistan.[78]

Two months later, terrorists carried out a series of deadly bombings in Morocco and Saudi Arabia, presumably in response to bin Laden's directive. In Morocco, suicide bombers targeted Western and Jewish interests, killing forty-four people; in Saudi Arabia they struck a Western housing complex that took thirty-four lives, including eight Americans. Although no group took credit for the attacks, Moroccan officials linked the bombings in their country to al-Qaeda. The news seemed to suggest the terrorist organization was alive and well and that its leader was still committed to taking the fight to his enemy—even while on the run. Then, on September 10, 2003, one day before the second anniversary of the terrorist attacks on America, Al-Jazeera broadcast the first new video of bin Laden in nearly two years. U.S. authorities believed the purpose of the video was to bolster morale among his operatives. Some analysts, however, suggested that the war against al-Qaeda, which began in the mountains of Afghanistan but also included the freezing of terrorists' bank accounts around the world, had been more effective than the subsequent successful attacks by terrorists seemed to suggest. Terrorism expert David E. Kaplan gives this inside perspective on the damage that has been inflicted on the terrorist network:

> Al-Qaeda's wounds run deep. Over half of its key operational leaders are out of action, officials [say]. Its top leaders are increasingly isolated and on the run. Al-Qaeda's Afghan sanctuary is largely gone. Its military commander is dead. Its chief of operations sits in prison, as do some 3,000 associates from around the world.[79]

The Threat Remains

The situation within Afghanistan did not seem quite as promising. Although Rums-feld declared an end to major combat operations in Afghanistan on May 1, 2003, just over one month later, U.S. soldiers clashed with Taliban troops in a fierce firefight near Spinboldak. Forty Taliban rebels were killed, the most since Operation Anaconda more than one year earlier. The violent uprising showed that the Taliban rebels were unwilling to quit the fight. In fact the radical movement was seen as gaining momentum in tribal and refugee settlements just across

The Land Mine Mess

Afghanistan is thought to be the most heavily land-mined country in the world. Soviet troops left behind hundreds of thousands of mines they buried there during their ten-year occupation of the country. In the 1990s, as Afghan warlords fought bitterly with one another over control of the country, many more mines were buried. While thousands have been removed, those that remain pose a danger to the Afghan people. Children who have accidentally stepped on mines while playing have been severely injured or even killed.

The United Nations has mandated mine-clearing programs, but the most optimistic estimates say that will take years. Coalition forces are doing their part to speed up the process. The U.S. Army's 710th Ordnance Company (Explosive Ordnance Disposal, or EOD), together with the Canadian army EOD, is working hard to destroy the mines. Adding to their workload is the removal of small, unexploded cluster bomb canisters scattered across parts of the country. The bombs pose a significant risk to children because the canisters that house the explosives resemble a yellow soda can, and they can be set off simply by moving them.

the border in Pakistan, planning for a possible uprising against U.S. and coalition forces. Some Afghans even continued to long for their return. "There will be fighting until the Taliban get power again," exclaimed Nur Muhammed, an Afghan shopkeeper. "God willing, they will force those infidels [U.S.-led coalition] out of the country."[80]

Compounding the security problems in Afghanistan was the fact that, by early summer, attempts to build a national military and a police force had progressed slower than anticipated, and regional warlords were continuing their tribal disputes. Help may be on the way. The international community has pledged not only peacekeeping troops to Afghanistan but also money to help rebuild the battered nation. Countries around the world have promised $4.5 billion in aid to rebuild, with the United States contributing the most, at more than $820 million. But those figures represent a fraction of the amount the U.S. government alone pledged to rebuild Iraq following the war in that country. Some observers, skeptical of American motives, see the imbalance stemming from Iraq being the second leading oil producer in the world and Afghanistan possessing scant natural resources. Still, observers say even the aid that has been promised can make a difference in the war-torn country if it is targeted toward rebuilding key infrastructure, such as dams, roads, and cities. The projects, they contend, will create needed jobs and help to stabilize and modernize a nation that has until recently lived in the nineteenth century. Other experts see national security as the crucial factor in securing peace, but it will depend on a strong commitment from other nations. The opinion of retired U.S. Army lieutenant colonel Robert L. Maginniss is one shared by many. He warns:

Afghanistan won't be tamed in a year, or two. The United States will be in that country for, at minimum, a decade, with little hope the land will evolve into a safe place for families and commerce. . . . Absolutely more security is needed before Afghanistan can turn the corner from its chaotic past. The world community must provide that security, enough to stabilize every region of the country. Otherwise, Afghanistan is more than likely to keep sliding back into the pit of terrorists from which it is so desperately trying to emerge.[81]

⭐ Notes ⭐

Introduction: The First Battle in the War Against Terrorism

1. Quoted in *Talk of the Nation*, "Analysis: Pentagon Briefing from Secretary Rumsfeld and General Myers," National Public Radio, October 18, 2001. www.npr.org.
2. Quoted in Mark Mazzetti, "Exclusive: How Special Ops Forces Are Hunting al-Qaeda," *U.S. News & World Report*, February 25, 2002.
3. Stephen Tanner, *Afghanistan: A Military History from Alexander the Great to the Fall of the Taliban*. New York: Da Capo, 2002, p. 324.

Chapter 1: Afghanistan: A Land of Chaos and Conflict

4. Neamatollah Nojumi, *The Rise of the Taliban in Afghanistan*. New York: Palgrave, 2002, pp. 2–3.
5. Nojumi, *The Rise of the Taliban in Afghanistan*, p. 6.
6. Nikita Khrushchev, *Khrushchev Remembers*. Boston: Little, Brown, 1971, pp. 560–62.
7. Nancy Peabody Newell and Richard Newell, *The Struggle for Afghanistan*. Ithaca, NY: Cornell University Press, 1981, pp. 72–75.
8. Ralph H. Magnus and Eden Naby, *Afghanistan: Mullah, Marx, and Mujahid*. Boulder, CO: Westview, 2002, p. 63.

9. Ahmed Rashid, *Jihad: The Rise of Militant Islam in Central Asia*. New Haven, CT: Yale University Press, 2002, p. 44.
10. Martin McCauley, *Afghanistan and Central Asia: A Modern History*. London: Longman, 2002, p. 19.
11. BBC News, "Analysis: Who Are the Taleban?" December 20, 2000. www.bbc.co.uk.
12. M.J. Gohari, *The Taliban Ascent to Power*. Oxford: Oxford University Press, 1999, p. 102.

Chapter 2: Osama bin Laden and al-Qaeda Terror Network

13. Quoted in Jason Burke, "The Making of Osama bin Laden," *Observer* (London), October 28, 2001. http://observer.guardian.co.uk.
14. Burke, "The Making of Osama bin Laden."
15. Quoted in *Frontline*, "A Biography of Osama," PBS, 2001. www.pbs.org.
16. Rohan Gunaratna, *Inside al Qaeda: Global Network of Terror*. New York: Columbia University Press, 2002, p. 20.
17. Quoted in Robert Fisk, "Talks With Osama bin Laden." *The Nation*, September 21, 1993, pp. 24–27.
18. John Barry, Christopher Dickey, and Steve Levine, "Making a Symbol of Terror," *Newsweek*, March 1, 1999, p. 40.
19. Gunaratna, *Inside al Qaeda*, p. 28.

20. Quoted in BBC News, "The UK's bin Laden Dossier in Full," October 4, 2001. www.bbc.co.uk.

21. Quoted in Barry, Dickey, and Levine, "Making a Symbol of Terror," p. 40.

22. Quoted in *Frontline*, "Interview: Osama bin Laden," PBS, May 1998. www.pbs.org.

23. Quoted in Mitch Frank, *Understanding September 11th: Answering Questions About the Attacks on America*. New York: Penguin, 2002, p. 23.

Chapter 3: The United States Mobilizes for War

24. Quoted in Terry Moran, "A Presidency Changed, One Year Ago Today," ABC News, September 11, 2002. www.abcnews.com.

25. George W. Bush, address to the nation, September 11, 2001, Office of the Press Secretary. www.whitehouse.gov.

26. U.S. Newswire, "Transcript of Sept. 20 Remarks of President Bush and Prime Minister Tony Blair," September 20, 2001. www.whitehouse.gov.

27. Quoted in Reuters, "Bush Address at Washington Memorial Service," September 14, 2001. www.whitehouse.gov.

28. Quoted in Bill Sammon, *Fighting Back*. Washington, DC: Regnery, 2002, p. 189.

29. George W. Bush, address to a joint session of Congress and the American people, September 20, 2001, Office of the Press Secretary. www.whitehouse.gov.

30. Quoted in *NewsHour with Jim Lehrer*, "How Wide a War?" PBS, September 26, 2001, Online NewsHour. www.pbs.org.

31. United Nations, "Security Council Committee Established Pursuant to Resolution 1373 (2001) Concerning Counter-Terrorism," September 28, 2001. www.un.org.

32. Bush, address to a joint session of Congress and the American people, September 20, 2001.

33. CNN, "Gen. Wesley Clark: U.S. Military Retaliation Options," September 18, 2001. www.cnn.com.

34. Quoted in Peter Baker and Molly Moore, "Anti-Taliban Rebels Eager to Join U.S. Retaliation," *Washington Post*, September 24, 2001.

35. Bob Woodward, *Bush at War*. New York: Simon & Schuster, 2002, p. 40.

36. Bush, address to a joint session of Congress and the American people, September 20, 2001.

37. Quoted in Michael A. Lev, "Bin Laden Backers Start Their War with Words," *Chicago Tribune*, September 23, 2001.

38. Quoted in Sayed Salahuddin, "Taliban Have Hidden bin Laden for his Safety," Reuters, September 30, 2001.

39. Quoted in Jack Kelley, "Special Forces Hunt bin Laden," *USA Today*, September 28, 2001.

40. Quoted in Kelley, "Special Forces Hunt bin Laden."

41. Quoted in Amir Zia, "Taliban 11th Hour Appeal Fails," Associated Press, October 7, 2001, AP Online. www.ap.org.

Chapter 4: Operation Enduring Freedom Begins

42. Quoted in Sammon, *Fighting Back*, p. 227.

43. George W. Bush, address to the nation, October 7, 2001, Office of the Press Secretary. www.whitehouse.gov.

44. Quoted in Charles Aldinger, "Rumsfeld Cautious About Quick Victory in Attacks," Reuters, October 8, 2001.

45. Quoted in Omar Shama, "Bin Laden Makes Tape Praising Attacks," Associated Press, October 8, 2001, AP Online. www.ap.org.

46. Quoted in Shama, "Bin Laden Makes Tape Praising Attacks."

47. Quoted in Thomas E. Ricks and Vernon Loeb, "Initial Aim Is Hitting Taliban's Defenses; U.S. Also Seeks Data as bin Laden Reacts," *Washington Post*, October 8, 2001.

48. Quoted in *Time*, "Opening Up the Psy-Ops War: The U.S. Goes on the Offensive for the Hearts and Minds of Afghans," October 16, 2001, Time Online Edition. www.time.com.

49. George W. Bush, White House press conference, October 15, 2001, Office of the Press Secretary. www.whitehouse.gov.

50. Quoted in Fox News, "Special Report with Brit Hume," October 8, 2001. www.foxnews.com

51. Robin Moore, *The Hunt for bin Laden: Task Force Dagger*. New York: Random House, 2003, p. 19.

52. Moore, *The Hunt for bin Laden*, p. 63.

53. R.W. Apple Jr., "A Military Quagmire Remembered: Afghanistan as Vietnam," *New York Times*, October 31, 2001, p. B1.

54. Quoted in Bob Woodward, "Doubts and Debate Before Victory over Taliban; Bush Demanded Advisers Be Patient," *Washington Post*, November 18, 2002, p. A01.

Chapter 5: The Sudden Taliban Collapse

55. Quoted in Global Security Newswire, "U.S. Explains Ramadan Bombing to Afghans." November 6, 2001. www.nti.org.

56. Quoted in *All Things Considered*, "Analysis: U.S. More than Doubles Special Forces Numbers Operating in Afghanistan," National Public Radio, November 6, 2001. www.npr.org.

57. Quoted in Dana Priest, "Team 555 Shaped a New Way of War: Special Forces and Smart Bombs Turned Tide and Routed Taliban," *Washington Post*, April 3, 2002, p. A01.

58. Weekly Compilation of Presidential Documents, "Remarks Following Discussions with President Perez Musharraf of Pakistan . . . ," November 19, 2001, p. 1642.

59. Quoted in Scott Peterson, "Despite U.S., Afghan Rebels Approach Kabul," *Christian Science Monitor*, November 13, 2001, p. 1.

60. Moore, *The Hunt for bin Laden*, p. 101.

61. Quoted in *Fox News Sunday*, "Political Headlines; Interview with Colin Powell," November 18, 2001. www.foxnews.com.

62. Justin Huggler, "The Castle of Death," *Independent* (London), November 30, 2001, pp. 1, 7.

63. Quoted in *All Things Considered*, "Profile: U.S. Sends Marines to Set Up Outpost near Kandahār in Southern Afghanistan," National Public Radio, November 26, 2001. www.npr.org.

Chapter 6: The Hunt for Osama bin Laden

64. U.S. Department of Defense, "Gen. Myers Interview with *Fox Sunday Morning*," December 9, 2001. www.defenselink.mil.

65. Moore, *The Hunt for bin Laden*, p. 241.

66. Quoted in Philip Smucker, "After Tora Bora, U.S. Hunts Alone," *Christian Science Monitor*, January 28, 2002, p. 1.

67. *Weekly Compilation of Presidential Documents*, "Remarks Welcoming General Tommy R. Franks and an Exchange with Reporters in Crawford, Texas," December 31, 2001, p. 1,828.

68. Quoted in IslamOnline, "General Franks: More 'Operation Anacondas' to Come," March 18, 2002. www.IslamOnline.net

69. Quoted in Tanalee Smith, "General: U.S. Troops Making Headway Against al-Qaida," Associated Press, August 30, 2002. www.azcentral.com.

70. U.S. Department of Defense, "Message from the Chairman of the Joint Chiefs of Staff on the One-Year Anniversary of Operation," October 7, 2002. www.defenselink.mil.

Chapter 7: The Struggle for Peace

71. Quoted in *All Things Considered*, "Analysis: Hamid Karzai Sworn In as Afghanistan's New President on the Last Day of the Loya Jirga, National Public Radio, June 19, 2002. www.npr.org.

72. Quoted in *NewsHour with Jim Lehrer*, "Keeping the Peace," PBS, November 21, 2002, Online NewsHour. www.pbs.org.

73. Edward Girardet, "A New Day in Kabul," *National Geographic*, December 2002, p. 95.

74. Quoted in Sonya Ross, "Afghan President to U.S.: 'Don't Forget Us If Iraq Happens,'" Associated Press, February 26, 2003.

75. Quoted in Scott Baldaut, "Despite Iraq, U.S. Raising Its Presence in Kabul." *Christian Science Monitor*, February 20, 2003, p. 1.

76. Quoted in Marie Schult, "Operation Valiant Strike," *Army*, May 2003.

77. Quoted in Reuters, "White House Doubts Report on Bin Laden's Sons," March 7, 2003. www.freerepublic.com.

78. Quoted in *Halifax Herald Limited*, "Bin Laden Triggered Bombings in Tape," May 18, 2003. www.herald.ns.ca.

79. David E. Kaplan, "Playing Offense: The Inside Story of How U.S. Terrorist Hunters Are Going After al Qaeda," *U.S. News & World Report*, June 2, 2003, p.20.

80. Quoted in Carlotta Gall, "Taliban Gather Openly in Pakistan and Talk of Return," *International Herald Tribune*, May 8, 2003.

81. Quoted in Robert L. Maginness, "Outside View: Afghanistan Unraveled," United Press International, August 8, 2002.

☆ For Further Reading ☆

Books

David Bohrer, *America's Special Forces: Weapons, Missions, and Training*. Osceola, WI: MBI, 1998. This pre–Operation Enduring Freedom volume offers a rare look into the secret world of the U.S. military's elite fighters—the army's Green Berets and Rangers, Marine Force Recon, navy SEALs, and USAF Special Ops.

CBS News, *What We Saw: The Events of September 11*. New York: Simon & Schuster, 2002. A collection of media excerpts reconstructing the tragic events of September 11, 2001.

Editors of *Der Spiegel* magazine, *Inside 9-11: What Really Happened*. New York: St. Martin's, 2002. This extensive volume includes a detailed chronology of the tragic events of September 11, 2001.

Editors of *Life* magazine, *One Nation: America Remembers September 11, 2001*. New York: Little, Brown, 2001. A moving account of the terrorist attacks on America, complete with an introduction by former New York mayor Rudy Giuliani and a wide range of photographs and essays.

Leila Merrell Foster, *Enchantment of the World: Afghanistan*. New York: Childrens, 1996. A fact-filled look at Afghanistan, its diverse peoples, unique culture, and troubled history.

Mitch Frank, *Understanding September 11th: Answering Questions About the Attacks on America*. New York: Penguin, 2002. Provides a helpful framework for understanding the possible motivation behind the terrorist attacks and the key issues and players surrounding them, including Osama bin Laden, al-Qaeda and the Taliban, the hijackers, and radical Islam.

Websites

CBS News (www.cbsnews.com). This highly interactive website covers the air and ground campaigns in Afghanistan through the first nine weeks of the war.

Global Security (www.globalsecurity.org). An outstanding source of information for Operation Enduring Freedom, including deployments, individual operations, weapons, maps, and more.

★ Works Consulted ★

Books

M.J. Gohari, *The Taliban Ascent to Power.* Oxford: Oxford University Press, 1999. An excellent overview of the Taliban's radical doctrine, swift rise to power in Afghanistan, and turbulent relationship with the West.

Rohan Gunaratna, *Inside al Qaeda: Global Network of Terror.* New York: Columbia University Press, 2002. An extensive look at the inner workings of the terrorist organization, including its origins, ideology, command structure, and tactics.

Nikita Khrushchev, *Khrushchev Remembers.* New York: Little, Brown, 1970. This autobiography traces Khrushchev's life from childhood to his days as Soviet leader during the Cold War.

Ralph H. Magnus and Eden Naby, *Afghanistan: Mullah, Marx, and Mujahid.* Boulder, CO: Westview, 2002. The authors present an insightful account of Afghanistan's volatile history, from the struggle with Britain in the Great Game to the Taliban's role in the terrorist attacks on America.

Martin McCauley, *Afghanistan and Central Asia: A Modern History.* London: Longman, 2002. A useful study of Afghanistan, its Central Asian neighbors, and the central issues that affect them: Islam, money, the Taliban, and international terrorism.

Robin Moore, *The Hunt for bin Laden: Task Force Dagger.* New York: Random House, 2003. This compelling volume details the ground operations of the elite U.S. Special Forces as they fought the Taliban and attempted to capture the al-Qaeda terrorist leader.

Nancy Peabody Newell and Richard Newell, *The Struggle for Afghanistan.* Ithaca, NY: Cornell University Press, 1981. A detailed analysis of the 1979 Soviet invasion of Afghanistan and its immediate aftermath.

Neamatollah Nojumi, *The Rise of the Taliban in Afghanistan.* New York: Palgrave, 2002. The author, a former member of the anti-Soviet mujahideen, offers an inside perspective of how decades of conflict led to the rise of militant Islam in Afghanistan.

Ahmed Rashid, *Jihad: The Rise of Militant Islam in Central Asia.* New Haven, CT: Yale University Press, 2002. A comprehensive study of the increase in Islamic fundamentalism in Central Asia after the collapse of Soviet communism.

Bill Sammon, *Fighting Back.* Washington, DC: Regnery, 2002. A generally favorable view of President Bush's leadership in the days and months following the terrorist attacks of September 11, 2001.

Stephen Tanner, *Afghanistan: A Military History from Alexander the Great to the Fall of the*

Taliban. New York: Da Capo, 2002. An excellent summary of Afghanistan's major historical conflicts.

Bob Woodward, *Bush at War.* New York: Simon & Schuster, 2002. A behind-the-scenes look at the Bush White House through the first year of military operations in Afghanistan and the months leading up to the conflict in Iraq.

Periodicals

Charles Aldinger, "Rumsfeld Cautious About Quick Victory in Attacks," Reuters, October 8, 2001.

R.W. Apple Jr., "A Military Quagmire Remembered: Afghanistan as Vietnam," *New York Times,* October 31, 2001.

Peter Baker and Molly Moore, "Anti-Taliban Rebels Eager to Join U.S. Retaliations," *Washington Post,* September 24, 2001.

Scott Baldauf, "All Smiles, Afghan Girls Go Back to School," *Christian Science Monitor,* December 3, 2001.

John Barry, Christopher Dickey, and Steve Levine, "Making a Symbol of Terror," *Newsweek,* March 1, 1999.

Jason Burke, "The Making of Osama bin Laden," *Observer* (London), October 28, 2001.

Robert Fisk, "Anti-Soviet Warrior Puts His Army on the Road to Peace," *Independent* (London), December 6, 1993.

Carlotta Gall, "Taliban Gather Openly in Pakistan and Talk of Return," *International Herald Tribune,* May 8, 2003.

Edward Girardet, "A New Day in Kabul," *National Geographic,* December 2002.

Guardian (Manchester), "Full Text of Tony Blair's Speech," September 11, 2001.

Zeeshan Haider, "Bin Laden Sons Said Hurt, 9 Killed in Afghan Raid," Reuters, March 7, 2003.

Halifax Herald Limited, "Bin Laden Triggered Bombings in Tape," May 8, 2003.

John Hendren and Maura Reynolds, "The U.S. Bomb That Nearly Killed Karzai," *Los Angeles Times,* March 27, 2002.

Justin Huggler, "The Castle of Death," *Independent* (London), November 30, 2001.

David E. Kaplan, "Playing Offense: The Inside Story of How U.S. Terrorist Hunters Are Going After al Qaeda," *U.S. News & World Report,* June 2, 2003.

Jack Kelley, "Special Forces Hunt bin Laden," *USA Today,* September 28, 2001.

Michael A. Lev, "Bin Laden Backers Start Their War with Words," *Chicago Tribune,* September 23, 2001.

Robert L. Maginniss, "Outside View: Afghanistan Unraveled," United Press International, August 8, 2002.

Mark Mazzetti, "Exclusive: How Special Ops Forces Are Hunting al-Qaeda," *U.S. News & World Report,* February 25, 2002.

Scott Peterson, "Despite U.S., Afghan Rebels Approach Kabul," *Christian Science Monitor,* November 13, 2001.

Dana Priest, "Team 555 Shaped a New Way of War," *Washington Post,* April 3, 2002.

Reuters, "Bush Address at Washington Memorial Service," September 14, 2001.

———, "Bush, Musharraf Oppose Afghan Rebels in Kabul," November 10, 2001.

Reuters Business Report, "Bush Announces $320 Million in Afghanistan Aid," October 4, 2001.

Thomas E. Ricks and Vernon Loeb, "Initial Aim Is Hitting Taliban's Defenses; U.S. Also Seeks Data as bin Laden Reacts," *Washington Post*, October 8, 2001.

Sonya Ross, "Afghan President to U.S.: 'Don't Forget Us If Iraq Happens,'" Associated Press, February 26, 2003.

Ali Ahmed Safi, "Despite Iraq, U.S. Raising Its Presence in Kabul," *Christian Science Monitor*, February 20, 2003.

Sayed Salahuddin, "Taliban Have Hidden bin Laden for His Safety," Reuters, September 30, 2001.

Marie Schult, "Operation Valiant Strike," *Army*, May 2003.

Katharine Q. Seelye, "Regretful Lindh Gets 20 Years in Taliban Case," *New York Times*, October 5, 2002.

Tanalee Smith, "U.S. Military Commander Says U.S. Troops in Afghanistan Chipping Away at al-Qaida," Associated Press, August 30, 2002.

Philip Smucker, "After Tora Bora, U.S. Hunts Alone," *Christian Science Monitor*, January 28, 2002.

U.S. Newswire, "Transcript of Sept. 20 Remarks of President Bush and Prime Minister Tony Blair," September 20, 2001.

Washington Post, "U.S. Commander Shuns Spotlight; Franks Criticized on Pace of War," November 11, 2001.

Washington Times, "Ramadan Respite Lacks Precedent," November 11, 2001.

Weekly Compilation of Presidential Documents, "Remarks Welcoming General Tommy R. Franks and an Exchange with Reporters in Crawford, Texas," December 31, 2001.

Michael Wines, "Caves and Tunnels: Heavily Fortified 'Ant Farms' Deter bin Laden's Pursuers," *New York Times*, November 26, 2001.

Bob Woodward, "Doubts and Debate Before Victory over Taliban; Bush Demanded Advisers Be Patient," *Washington Post*, November 18, 2002.

Internet Sources

ABC News, "Afghan Care Packages: U.S. Drops Food in Afghanistan," October 8, 2001. www.abcnews.com.

All Things Considered, "Analysis: Hamid Karzai Sworn In as Afghanistan's New President on the Last Day of the Loya Jirga," National Public Radio, June 19, 2002. www.npr.org.

———, "Analysis: U.S. More than Doubles Special Forces Numbers Operating in Afghanistan," National Public Radio, November 6, 2001. www.npr.org.

———, "Profile: U.S. Sends Marines to Set Up Outpost Near Kandahār in Southern Afghanistan," National Public Radio, November 26, 2001. www.npr.org.

Associated Press, "Carrier *Roosevelt*, Dozens of Attack Jets Part of 'Repositioning,'" September 20, 2001.

BBC News, "Analysis: Who Are the Taleban?" December 20, 2000. www.bbc.co.uk.

———, "The UK's Bin Laden Dossier in Full," October 4, 2001. www.bbc.co.uk.

George W. Bush, address to a joint session of Congress and the American people, September 20, 2001, Office of the Press Secretary. www.whitehouse.gov.

————, address to the nation, September 11, 2001, Office of the Press Secretary. www.whitehouse.gov.

————, address to the nation, October 7, 2001, Office of the Press Secretary. www.whitehouse.gov.

————, remarks by the president at swearing-in of Tom Ridge, secretary of the Department of Homeland Security, January 24, 2003, Office of the Press Secretary. www.whitehouse.gov.

————, White House press conference, October 15, 2001, Office of the Press Secretary. www.whitehouse.gov.

CNN, "Gen. Wesley Clark: U.S. Military Retaliation Options," September 18, 2001. www.cnn.com.

Fox News, "Special Report with Brit Hume," October 8, 2001. www.foxnews.com.

Fox News Sunday, "Political Headlines: Interview with Colin Powell," November 18, 2001. www.foxnews.com.

Frontline, "A Biography of Osama," PBS, 2001. www.pbs.org.

————, "Interview: Osama bin Laden," PBS, May 1998. www.pbs.org.

IslamOnline, "General Franks: More 'Operation Anacondas' to Come," March 18, 2002. www.islamonline.net.

Terry Moran, "A Presidency Changed, One Year Ago Today," ABC News, September 11, 2002. www.abcnews.com.

NewsHour with Jim Lehrer, "How Wide a War?" PBS, September 26, 2001, Online NewsHour. www.pbs.org.

————, "Keeping the Peace," PBS, November 21, 2002, Online NewsHour. www.pbs.org.

Omar Shama, "Bin Laden Makes Tape Praising Attacks," Associated Press, October 8, 2001, AP Online. www.ap.org.

Talk of the Nation, "Analysis: Pentagon Briefing from Secretary Rumsfeld and General Myers," National Public Radio, October 18, 2001. www.npr.org.

Time, "Opening Up the PsyOps War: The U.S. Goes on the Offensive for the Hearts and Minds of Afghans," October 16, 2001, Time Online Edition. www.time.com.

United Nations, "Security Council Committee Established Pursuant to Resolution 1373 (2001) Concerning Counter-Terrorism," September 28, 2001. www.un.org.

U.S. Department of Defense, "Gen. Myers Interview with *Fox Sunday Morning*," December 9, 2001. www.defenselink.mil.

————, "Message from the Chairman of the Joint Chiefs of Staff on the One-Year Anniversary of Operation," October 7, 2002. www.defenselink.mil.

————, "Secretary Rumsfeld Remarks at Stakeout Outside ABC TV," October 28, 2001. www.defenselink.mil.

————, "Transcript of Osama bin Laden Video Tape," December 13, 2001. www.defenselink.mil.

Amir Zia, "Taliban 11th Hour Appeal Fails," Associated Press, October 7, 2001, AP Online. www.ap.org.

✯ Index ✯

★ Picture Credits ★

Cover: Jim Holland/Reuters/Landov

© AFP/CORBIS

© AP Wide World, 17, 19, 22, 29, 32, 41, 43, 48, 63, 69, 74

Bernard/CORBIS SYGMA, 57

Department of Defense photo by Petty Officer First Class Greg Messier, U.S. Navy, 10

Department of Defense photo by R.D. Ward, 60, 84

Department of Defense Photo by Sgt. First Class William A. Jones, U.S. Army, 89

Department of Defense photo by Sgt. Kevin P. Bell, U.S. Army, 86

Anton Meres/Reuters/Landov, 92

Corinne Dufka/Reuters/Landov, 32, 35

Reuters/Landov, 27, 46, 80, 91

U.S. Air Force photo by Tech. Sgt. Scott Reed, 62

U.S. Navy photo by Photographer's Mate First Class Tim Turner, 11

U.S. Navy photo by Photographer's Mate Third Class Philip A. McDaniel, 51

⭐ About the Author ⭐

Raymond H. Miller is the author of more than fifty nonfiction children's books, covering topics in American history, endangered animals, and sports heroes. He lives in Orlando, Florida, with his wife and two daughters.